Being a
Successful
Principal

Being a Successful Principal

Riding the Wave of Change Without Drowning

David R. Schumaker
William A. Sommers

CORWIN PRESS, INC.
A Sage Publications Company
Thousand Oaks, California

For information:

Corwin Press, Inc.
A Sage Publications Company
2455 Teller Road
Thousand Oaks, California 91320
E-mail: order@corwinpress.com

Sage Publications Ltd.
6 Bonhill Street
London EC2A 4PU
United Kingdom

Sage Publications India Pvt. Ltd.
M-32 Market
Greater Kailash I
New Delhi 110 048 India

Printed in the United States of America

Library of Congress Cataloging-in-Publication Data

Schumaker, David R.
  Being a successful principal: Riding the wave of change without drowning / by David R. Schumaker and William A. Sommers.
    p. cm.
  Includes bibliographical references (p. 170) and index.
  ISBN 0-8039-6768-3 (cloth: acid-free paper)
  ISBN 0-8039-6769-1 (pbk.: acid-free paper)
    1. School principals—United States. 2. School management and organization—United States. I. Sommers, William A. II. Title.
  LB2831.92 .S37 2000
  371.2'012—dc21   00-009510

This book is printed on acid-free paper.

01   02   03   04   05   06   10   9   8   7   6   5   4   3   2   1

Production Editor: Denise Santoyo
Editorial Assistant: Cindy Bear
Typesetter/Designer: Barbara Burkholder
Indexer: Pamela Van Huss

Contents

Preface

This book is for principals and aspiring principals. We feel schools should be true learning communities, and we wish to share our experiences as principals who have been there and found some ways to lead schools and to create synchronistic thinking environments. Anyone reading this book will soon realize that it is not theory; it is reality based on our experiences of what works and what doesn't work. It is written out of a love of children and educators. We wanted to share our experiences with others in a similar position. It is not the end all, but it will make you think, maybe laugh, and you may pick up some ideas and hints that will help you be the best you can be.

WHY WE WROTE THIS BOOK

We were sitting in a coffee shop in Vancouver, British Columbia, reflecting on the National Staff Development Conference we had just attended. We have both been to many conferences, looking for ideas, inspiration, and possibilities that would help us be effective principals. We were comparing notes on what we had learned to date and the books we had read when we came to a realization. We concluded that of all the presentations and books we had read very few truly shared the day-to-day reality of the job of being a principal.

Both of us are journal keepers, and sitting there talking we decided that we had the experiences and the stories to write a book about being a principal from our own reflections. We also thought that this would not be written in the typical formal academic style that requires the reader to plod through from page 1 to the end.

Rather, it would be a readable journal that could be picked up, opened to any chapter, and read. It would be the book that we wished we could have had when we began our careers as administrators.

This book is for you, the principal. Because you are the boss, your job is one of isolation and loneliness among a crowd of adults and children. Principals must stay close to home during the school year, so they rely on publications for much of their professional growth. They have a wide choice of everything from books for educators written by authors from the world of business, such as *The Empowered Manager* (1987) by Peter Block or Lee Bolman and Terrence Deal's (1995) *Leading With Soul*. There are also books on leadership, such as *Leaders* by Warren Bennis and Burt Nanus (1985) and *Why Leaders Can't Lead* by Warren Bennis (1989). There are also books by professional educators and educational researchers—*The Constructivist Leader* by Linda Lambert and colleagues (1995) and *Punished by Rewards* by Alfie Kohn (1993) are examples. There are many books on theory and specific practice, but few are written from the perspective of the day-to-day experience of being a principal by someone who has been there. It is a report of survival by natural selection as the authors evolved ideas from theory into practice.

AUDIENCE AND PURPOSE

Who Should Read This Book

Nick Saban, a football coach at Michigan State University, once said, "I don't need advice on Sunday morning. I know what to do then. If you want to help me, tell me what to do within 15 seconds on the sideline on Saturday. That is when I need the help."

This book is for administrators, aspiring administrators, or anyone interested in how schools are run on a day-to-day basis. It is especially written for principals or past principals, who will identify with the stress and struggle of school leadership, and for those people interested in leading from a constructivist philosophy who want to encourage a collaborative approach to school management that we believe creates an environment of trust and involvement benefiting each child's learning.

Scope

Being a Successful Principal is full of experience that covers many aspects of being a principal in a shared-leadership school. It is not an all-encompassing work, but rather a collection of experiences.

Chapter 1: Communication—the Foundational Skill

It all starts with communication. Administrators cannot expect results if they cannot communicate what they want and how they want it done in a way that encourages others to listen and act. Trust is built through open and truthful communication. It is a two-way process. Administrators not only need to convey their message; they also need to listen to what is going on in and around their school. Listening is part of communication. Effective change is built on effective feedback.

Chapter 2: Trusting Yourself, Trusting Others

The principal is truly alone in the crowd. On a campus of 2,000 students or 200, complete with teachers, aides, classified staff, and parents, the principal is the only person at this level of responsibility—the principal has no equivalent colleague to act as a confidant; even his or her secretary is usually not a confidential secretary and belongs to the local bargaining unit. To everyone the principal encounters, he or she is the boss, leader, and symbol of authority. The principal is also the others' evaluator. It is essential that he or she can trust himself or herself to make quality decisions, to handle emergencies, to inspire others to be the best they can be, to name only a few qualities. The job is too big for one person, and as a result, if the job is to be done effectively, the principal has to trust that regulation of authority will result in good work without micromanaging. Building that rapport takes time and skill.

Chapter 3: Learning to Change (and Liking It)

"We are a good school, do we really need to change?" On my first day as principal of a middle school, a committee from the faculty met with me and explained that the school was once considered the worst in the country and now it was considered the best. They went on to tell me that they had worked hard to get where they were and they did not want me to change them. They had the "if it ain't broke, don't fix it" mentality. Clearly, if the school was to continue to be a leader it had to change and keep changing.

Chapter 4: Classrooms Are Not the Only Places to Learn

School should be an adventure. The idea that the classroom is where all learning takes place defies logic. In fact, often classroom learning is not "real-life" learning, and much of what goes on there is ignored and forgotten, for good reason, as the child grows, matures, and travels out into the world of work and family. Students learn constantly, and a good school uses all the resources on and off campus to provide a practical, real-life learning environment. From traveling schools, field trips, and business partnerships to the classified staff showing students how to fix a leaky pipe or plant a tree or students stopping on the way home to view local art in a coffee shop—this chapter deals with the practical experiences of making the best use of adventures outside the classroom and off the campus to promote learning. How does the administrator deal with the problems of liability, forming partnerships, and protecting children as they learn in nontraditional ways?

Chapter 5: Tsunami—Riding the Wave of Change Without Drowning

In California in 1996, the governor and legislature decided in late July to reduce the class size of Grades K through 2 from a ratio of approximately 30 to 1 to 20 to 1 by September. Talk about a tsunami! No district was prepared for this magnitude of change. Where do the classrooms come from? Where do we get qualified teachers? How do we move new green teachers up to speed in a few weeks? A good friend once told me that change was inevitable and growth was optional! Public schools are subject to change day in and day out. Whether it is a sudden storm, earthquake, or fire or merely the students' request for a special day to honor the fact that they have kept the campus clean for a month, it means dealing with change. Presently, public schools, facing the threat of vouchers, should be looking at themselves for areas in need of change to better serve their students.

Chapter 6: Mediating Conflict

When I was first teaching, my principal told me that his job was to "kick ass and take notes" (Theory X). Another principal told me that stress on a faculty was the best motivator to learn. Both were wrong. Even the best of us needs a coach—Jack Nicklaus himself has a coach—but the coaching we are talking about is quite different than most coaching concepts. In Cognitive Coaching©, the coach mediates the thinking for the person being coached. Even though we are each of us at the same time an individual and a part of something else, teachers usually see themselves as alone and without support. The act of mediative coaching can prepare teachers for those times when they are confronted by problems and away from instant help by enabling them to think through anticipated problems and give them a framework for self-coaching when the need arises.

Chapter 7: Standing Your Ground (Even in Quicksand)

Early in my administrative career, a seasoned teacher caught me alone in my office. It was my first year at the school and I was trying to avoid making a difficult decision. This teacher was involved with the decision, and after several days of my looking for a solution that would not hurt anyone's feelings she was in my face again. This time she said, "David, you have got to understand that you must make a decision, and until you do I am going to make your life hell!" With that, I said that the decision was "No!" She could not do what she wanted to do. She stood up, hugged me, and said, "Thank you. You have saved energy for both of us." Sooner or later, we have to exert the power of the office. Principals are ultimately responsible for everything on campus and must understand that they cannot please everyone. They can, however, make their feelings known without breaking trust and be able to maintain relationships with those disappointed by decisions.

Chapter 8: Assessing Students, Staff, and Schools

If you do not know where you have been, how can you tell where you are going? If you do not know where you are going, how will you know if you get there? There is a difference between feeling good and knowing you are good.

Chapter 9: Get a Life!

Remember that boss spelled backward is "double SOB!" It is easy to see how a person with increasing job demands and family responsibilities can become cranky and turn into the "boss spelled backward." The question becomes, "How does the administrator keep balance in his or her life?" In this chapter, we discuss ways that many administrators have found to keep their sanity in the face of overwhelming odds.

Chapter 10: The Principal's Toolbox: Anecdotes and Hints for Survival in a Cruel, Cruel World

Some things come to you as gifts. This chapter is filled with gifts and treasures that you can use for a variety of purposes. Many items here have evolved and will evolve more as they are used. The chapter is filled with ideas that you can use directly or that may cause you to think of a new idea and save you time and energy.

ACKNOWLEDGMENTS

There are many people who have touched both of our lives in our journey. We are a result of them. For Bill, I am indebted to Walter Gohman, who taught me to be a teacher; Art Costa, the reason I am still in education, who continues to challenge my learning and provides mentoring for me beyond anything I could imagine; Diane Zimmerman, whose coaching, thinking, and friendship continue to be a source of energy; Marney Wamsley, who taught me to be a more complete principal and continues to provide guidance for me; Michael Grinder, who won't let me settle for being good enough; Bob Chadwick, who taught me that conflict is and you can deal with it effectively; Ruby Payne, who keeps challenging me to think outside the box; Dave Schumaker, who continues to teach me about learning and education; and a host of others, including Marilyn Tabor, Bob Garmston, Jim Roussin, Michael Ayers, Tom Heuerman, and Skip Olsen.

For Dave, I am also indebted to Art Costa—without his coming into my professional life I would not have remained in education. I wish to thank Bob Garmston, Marty Krovetz, Suzanne Bailey, Bena Kallick, Marsha Speck, and Pat Wolf for their support and encouragement. I give special thanks to Don Rothwow and Lauren Hess, who convinced me that I could write. This book would not have been possible if it were not for the constant encouragement and clear editing by Pat Schumaker, Dave Schumaker's wife and partner. Her constant question, "Where's the beef?" forced me into clearer thinking and better writing. The book is completed and the marriage still intact. Bill and I are thankful for her dedication, help, and love.

David R. Schumaker
Hayfork, California

William A. Sommers
Edina, Minnesota

About the Authors

William A. Sommers, Ph.D., is Assistant Professor of educational leadership at Hamline University and is a junior high principal in Owatonna, Minnesota. For the past 10 years, he has been an associate trainer for the Institute of Intelligent Behavior based in Denver, Colorado, in Cognitive Coaching. He also conducts trainings in conflict management strategies, organizational development, understanding poverty, group dynamics facilitation, thinking skills, and brain research.

In addition to authoring many articles regarding coaching, assessment, and encouraging reflective thinking, he has been in K-12 education for 29 years as a teacher, an assistant principal, and a junior high and high school principal in suburban and urban schools. He has been an adjunct faculty member at the University of St. Thomas, the University of Minnesota, Capella University, and St. Mary's University.

He has just coauthored a book called *Living on a Tightrope: Survival Handbook for Principals,* which deals with the emotional intelligence of principals and new strategies required to manage and lead schools in the 21st century. He is currently working on another book on how to develop reflective practice in schools. He has presented to local, state, national, and international professional organizations; has conducted training in numerous state and national school districts; and works for several training organizations. He continues to work as a consultant in many districts because of the content he brings and the practitioner focus of his presentations.

xvi ◆ BEING A SUCCESSFUL PRINCIPAL

David R. Schumaker has been a public school teacher for 21 years, a principal of a high school and middle school for over 10 years, and a staff developer for 4 years as the Director of the Central Coast Consortium for Professional Development Region V, Santa Clara County Office of Education. As the director, he was one of 10 people working for the state of California helping to restructure high schools and high school teaching. His region covered the four counties Santa Cruz, Santa Clara, Monterey, and San Benito. Presently he is a full-time consultant.

As an associate of Dr. Art Costa, Dr. Bena Kallick, and Dr. David Hyerle, he has worked with teachers throughout the United States. He is also a Mentor on Assignment for the National School Conference Institute in Phoenix, Arizona. His workshops are in the areas of brain-based education, teaching strategies, assessment, Cognitive Coaching©, thinking skills, Habits of Mind, and Thinking Maps™. The emphasis of all of his workshops is on improving student learning across the curriculum. Currently, he lives in Northern California with his wife and best friend of 39 years, horses, dog, cats, chickens, and many other dependents. When not attending to his first passion, teaching, he drives horse and carriage for competition and longs to see his grandson more often.

1

Communication— the Foundational Skill

It all starts with communication—administrators cannot expect to be effective if they cannot communicate what they want and how they want it done in a way that encourages others to listen and act. Trust is built through open and truthful communication. It is a two-way process. Administrators not only need to convey their message; they also need to listen to what is going on in and around their school. Listening is part of communication. Effective change is built on effective feedback.

You have just hung up the phone; a warm glow flows through your body; you are excited, fearful, ecstatic, and exhilarated all at the same time. You just found out that after three days of progressive interviews with teachers, parents, businesspeople, administrators, and even some students, you have been selected as the new principal of Sunshine School. You immediately begin to think of all the great things you can accomplish and how you are not going to make the same mistakes you have seen other newly hired principals make.

Underneath all the excitement and opportunities you must realize that although you have not spent a single day or hour on the job and have only met a small fraction of the Sunshine School community, everyone there has a perception of what you are, what they expect you to be, and what you are expected to do—and all these perceptions are different. You are the target of a myriad of concepts about how you should do your job.

These perceptions are defined by the mistakes of the past administrators and the oaken bucket memories of the "perfect" ones. "Why, I remember back when I was a kid, we had a principal who

knew what a good school was and he . . ." Time dims the mistakes of
the past and you will be expected to meet everyone's expectations of
the perfect principal.

From the moment the immediate past principal resigned, everyone began to form a picture of who would take his or her place. The
board declared the position open and met with the recruiter to
define the perfect person for the job. The position was crafted by
groups of people from within and without the school culture, and
each person involved will help define you. You received the flyer
and built your application and responses to interview questions as a
result of their perceptions about the job and your perceptions about
how you could fit in. It will be impossible to meet all of those expectations and perceptions because your individual perceptions about
the job are as unique as everyone else's.

So, the dilemma that every new administrator faces is now
yours. How will you be the person everyone expects you to be? You
are expected to be the "educational leader." Will it be top down or
bottom up? Will it be inclusive or exclusive? How will you get your
message across? How will you get others to trust you?

To start with, if you try to attend to everyone's perception you
will develop a heavy case of multiple personality disorder and
everyone will soon discover that you are a phony. You have to be
your own person and be able to take the lead when you have to. I[1]
remember a principal who never had a mind of his own. He was
always asking for "input" on the resolution of some problem, and it
was not long before I figured out that the last person to get to him
with an idea just before he had to make the decision usually got his
or her way. I made a strong effort when I really cared about the decision to be that last person. I usually had things my way, and I had little respect for him.

Many newly hired administrators work from an old misconcep-
tion that a new leader can make major changes from the start and
the staff will forgive him or her for it. That they expect big changes
and will tolerate them is a myth. Although many teachers and community members accept that differences will come with a new
administrator in the district, they know what they want and they
hope to get it. Perceptions are facts in most minds.

A friend once told me that after he was hired he had a difficult
time discovering what the district expected, what was past history,

and what were the perceived rules of the new school. In other words, what was the school's culture? He said that it was not long before he tripped over things he did not know, and each misstep caused him problems. He described the experience as being like walking along a beach covered with seashells. Under some of the shells, important facts and fables of the school community were hidden from view. Every so often a wave would reach the beach with enough force to turn over some of the shells, revealing important information that he needed to do his job—revelations appearing unpredictably and randomly.

The obvious first step for the newly hired administrator becomes one of discovering what is considered rude and crude in your new district, what are the rules, and what others expect of you. How do you find out the facts? You start with questions, listen, take notes, think, reflect, and carry your journal and use it.

Feedback is what you are after. Without it you are steering in the fog. With it you can make adjustments and hope to improve what you are doing. The process is not a loop but a spiral, for a loop always brings you back to where you started and what good is that? Unless changes are made from the input received, a person is doomed to continue making the same mistakes again and again.

Spiral Feedback   Box 1.1

It was a cold gray foggy day. The fog was one of those thick, sticky ones that clings to everything it touches and drips like rain off the redwood trees, splashing on my windshield as we drove to the yacht harbor. Bob and I were out early and anticipating a fine day of fishing on Monterey Bay in a rented motorboat—no phones, no yard work, free.

"Don't get lost," were the final words hurled down out of the gray mist. Aldo, owner of the boat rental, retreated to the warmth of his restaurant and we arranged ourselves in the old green rowboat saturated with odors of the sea and the smell of gasoline and oil. Two sets of oars rested along the seats, and an old Evenrude 35 clung to the transom. It was one of those outboard motors that you sit alongside and run with a handle projecting at an angle out of the casing; twist it one way and it goes forward, the other and it reverses.

Bob took his place alongside the motor, assuming the job of captain, navigator, and chief engineer, as usual. I, always the mate, second mate to be sure when I was with Bob, sat in the bow and prepared to cast off.

"Cast off," rang the order.

"We're off," I responded as I coiled the rope on the floor and added, "Where are we going?"

"To the mile buoy!" he said, easing the boat away from the pier and heading into the thick curtain of fog out of the harbor.

I felt the boat begin that easy pitch fore and aft as we cut across the gentle waves approaching the harbor from the mouth of the twin jetties that marked the boundary of the channel. The red and green lights that marked the channel were easy to see as they emerged out of the fog. But I could hardly see the rocks of the jetty, and I wondered how Bob intended to find the mile buoy in this soup.

Bob eased the throttle up to full speed, and we plunged ahead into the mist as all traces of land vanished. We were alone in a world cloaked in a garment of fog so thick that our voices were muffled and the motor was hardly a purr. At times it was difficult to see Bob seated 12 feet away guiding us to our destination. At least he thought he was guiding us.

We ran smoothly on a timid sea, more like a millpond, smooth, glassy, almost waveless for about 15 minutes. All the time I was peering ahead with all my might as if I could poke my eyeballs through the curtain and see objects in time to warn the captain.

Suddenly, I was aware of a thin white horizontal line running across my field of view. I was somewhat disoriented by the cloud and wondered what it was and then, as if waking from a dream, realized it was the surf breaking on the beach alongside the harbor we left not long ago.

"Hard a-port!!" I cried in a sailorly fashion.

"Why?" he responded. Bob never did take advice from the crew well.

"Because we are going to hit the beach if . . ."

The boat suddenly lurched to port in a very tight turn, throwing everything off the seats and up against the starboard hull as Bob saw the danger we were in. I hung on for dear life and could see the sandy bottom of the bay through about 18 inches of water. We had almost beached the boat at full speed.

Without a word Bob headed back out away from the beach into the fog. The fog that now appeared even thicker. We had done what so many sailors, pilots, and hikers do when they are lost or deprived of a view; we sailed in a circle, an almost perfect circle.

The boat gained speed and once again we were alone in the mist. "Where are we going?" I asked.

"To the mile buoy!" he responded with as much conviction as the first time. Jaw set, arm held steady, and hand firmly gripping the throttle, he took us onward into the gloom.

Once again, after 15 or 20 minutes, unbelievably the beach appeared. Once again we veered away just in time. Once again we plunged into the fog toward the elusive "Mile buoy."

This time, however, I asked, "How are you going to find the buoy?"

Bob admitted that he didn't know and then requested my opinion.

I told him that I had a compass in my pack and maybe that would help.

"Why the hell didn't you tell me you had a compass?" he shouted.

"You never asked," I responded as we heard the bell on the mile buoy dead ahead, right where it should be.

Years later, I sit in my office thinking about that foggy day and feedback loops and spirals. Feedback loops are designed to just let you know where you are at the present and have little to do with where you are going if you don't act on the feedback received from them and adjust your course of action. We had sailed in a circle, twice, because we did nothing with the feedback we received from the first loop.

We started with a goal—to get to the mile buoy—and a purpose—to fish. We had our plan—exit the harbor and hold the boat steady in a straight line in the direction of the buoy. We took action by sailing and received feedback, or evidence, the appearance of the shoreline, which demonstrated that we were not on track toward our goal. We did nothing that first time to study, reflect, or evaluate; nor did we modify our actions based on new knowledge. As a result we achieved the same outcome as before—we almost hit the beach again.

Only after two loops did we take the proper steps to correct our course. We modified our actions by adding a compass. As a result we achieved our goal and enjoyed a fine day of fishing. (For a visual representation of this, see Figure 8.2.)

The story is funny, now that I look back on it. It was funny then—Bob and I laughed and laughed about how two grown men could make such a stupid mistake twice before we acted to change the outcome. Yet as I think about it today, how many schools are doing the same thing year after year?

Every year they take on passengers in September and set sail for the mile buoy, the goal of meaningful learning for each student, and hope that by June they all arrive safely, every student completing a successful voyage. Yet suddenly out of the fog, as they pull away from the dock, appear dropouts, failures, frustration, burnout, that same old feeling, and they realize that they have, once again, sailed in a futile circle.

It has been said, "If you always do what you did, you always get what you got." Feedback loops give us information on progress toward a goal. Feedback data from standardized tests or portfolios are of no consequence if no action is taken on what is learned. Without adjusting the course, we risk running aground.

Another thing that we do in education is to set different goals each year. We rarely build a new goal based on feedback on the results of pursuing the previous one.

For this reason, the process of "continuous growth through feedback spirals" becomes a more useful concept than a loop. In this process, a person or group starts by clarifying goals and purposes, then develops a plan to achieve those goals and purposes. Once the plan is in place, action and experimentation begin as progress is made toward the goal. Along the way, however, they must assess their progress, gathering evidence revealing how they well they are advancing. Once they have that information, they must study and reflect on it, evaluate their progress, and if they are not on target they must modify their actions based on the data. Once they have the goal in sight, they must revisit their intentions. Does achieving their goal really further their purpose, or do they need to change the goal and maybe even the purpose to get where they think they want to go? This continuous assessment moves people to their goals in an accurate and systematic process.

It is reported that when NASA sends a rocket to a faraway planet, 80% of the time it is off course and course corrections must be made based on feedback comparing trajectory to the path needed to hit the target.

At this point the spiral continues upward—revisit and clarify goals and purposes; plan, take action, and experiment; assess and gather evidence; study, reflect, and evaluate; modify actions based on new knowledge. A circle gets us nowhere; only by intelligently adjusting the course while under way will we ever be able to get all our children safely to port.

The day after I was hired as the new principal of New Brighton Middle School, I called the outgoing principal and asked him to set up a meeting for me with the entire staff. It was March, and I wanted to talk to them as soon as I could. The purpose was to begin the feedback process. I knew that they would want to see who I was and begin to get a feeling about how it would be to work with me. A new boss coming in is a high-stress time for some people. I also wanted to get to know the staff and begin a successful transition. During the first meeting it is important to listen and not to reveal too much about yourself. Many people will attempt to say what they think you want to hear, especially if they know your philosophy.

The meeting was held in the school library, and it was a jovial occasion. I had time to be introduced to everyone and make a couple of welcoming statements. I came prepared with some questions printed on sheets of paper for people to respond to. At the top of the page was a statement followed by three questions:

"Remember, none of us is as smart as all of us!" Please answer the following questions. There is only one rule: Opinions are fine but without supporting reasons for your opinions they are not very valuable to me. If you don't like something and want it changed, you must tell me why you don't like it and how you would change it.

1. What is the one thing you would never change about New Brighton Middle School?
2. What is the one thing you would change today about New Brighton Middle School?
3. Is there anything else you would like me to know?

It is not enough to just ask the questions. People want to give input and they do not expect to have everything go their way, but they need to see that something was accomplished with their input. I remember a principal that I had who would always ask us for input and then, after we spent valuable time giving it to him, he would leave the room saying, "Thank you for your input." That is all we would hear from him. It was not long before people quit giving him input.

I typed the answers to my questions in a two-column format with the paraphrased answers on the left and my response to them on the right. Although I consulted with the outgoing principal about the questions to get his input, all of the responses were mine. In some cases, what the staff wanted to do was not legal and I would tactfully explain why we could not do it. Others were good suggestions and could be acted on immediately. Some needed input from the entire staff, and I stated so. Finally, some were against my philosophy and I said so, explaining my personal educational perspective, and made no change.

One particular suggestion that was on many of the teachers' response forms still sticks in my mind. The school had a homeroom period of 12 minutes attached to the first period. The teachers did not like it and wanted it removed. I knew how effective a middle school advisory period could be for meeting some of the student's needs. I definitely wanted to implement an effective advisory period. On the response paper I wrote that I wanted to talk to them about the concept of an advisory instead of a homeroom.

When it came to any major change, I wanted to be sure that all of the staff would hear it from me personally. This meant a faculty meeting at a time I was sure everyone affected was there to meet with me in person so that I could explain myself and answer questions. If I had just responded in writing with an issued edict, many serious misunderstandings would develop. I always started those meetings with a statement of my rules for such decisions.

Rules for Shared Decision Making

- ◆ You have the right to participate.
- ◆ You have the right to make suggestions.
- ◆ You have the right to help us all decide how we will do something.
- ◆ You also have the responsibility to make an honest effort to try the new idea in a spirit of good faith and professionalism.
- ◆ You will most likely have the right to help us decide if we will continue with the new idea.
- ◆ *You do not, however, have the right to undermine our decision.*

These rules were passed to me by one of the very best administrators I have ever known. His name was Fernando Lopez, and I miss his fine advice.

Undermining can kill shared decision making. The process is often called the "parking lot meeting." The goal is to have the meeting *at* the meeting, not in the parking lot. You all know about it and how it happens. After a meeting where the teachers appear to be connected and agree with some proposal, they walk to their cars and in small groups begin to tell how they will subvert the decision. I did not tolerate it.

The way to prevent it from happening is multifaceted. The primary reason why people undermine is if they feel that their input is not heard or respected. When people feel that they cannot speak frankly about an idea or they have been coerced into something, the undermining will start. The real conversation will take place in the parking lot or on the phone and not in the meeting. Everyone needs to have equal time to speak on the topic during the meeting. To that end, a good meeting rule is that once a person has spoken to an issue that person may not speak again until everyone else has had time to speak.

Once we reach consensus, I expect everyone to participate in the implementation. If I hear of someone undermining us, I immediately find the person and confront him or her in a friendly way. I usually make sure the person is alone in his or her best place, such as a classroom, not my office. I say something like, "I hear that you are not happy with the staff's decision about . . . Is that true?" Usually that is all it takes, but sometimes, after listening, I have to remind the person of the rules and how the decision was made and that my door is always open. I then ask, "If you have concerns about *our* decision, why didn't you bring them up at the meeting or come and see me?"

COMMUNICATING WITH THE CENTRAL OFFICE

Remember Where Your Check Comes From

No superintendent wants to be surprised, no business manager wants you to spend money without authorization, and no central office wants to receive calls about you that the people there do not know about in advance.

Handling an Angry Parent   Box 1.2

I was sitting in my office at the end of a cold hard day when suddenly the door opened and a parent entered with my secretary following her mouthing, "I tried to stop her." I mouthed back that it was OK.

The parent was obviously upset. I asked her to sit down and tell me what was wrong. She stood there and began shouting, "Did you know that my daughter's sixth-grade teacher is pregnant?"

I admitted that I did know and that we were all happy for her.

She went on, "What are you going to do about it?" Not being sure where she was going with this question, I responded, "I am not sure what you mean. Help me understand why you seem so upset about her expecting."

She replied, "You're not going to let her teach children while she is pregnant, are you?"

The upshot was that she did not feel that pregnant women should be in public, let alone teach children. I explained that it was not only legal to be pregnant and in public, but that there were no codes that would have me remove her from the classroom.

She turned on her heels and yelled as she left the office, "If you won't do anything about it, I will take it up with your supervisor."

I could see her leaving the property and walking to the district office, only 200 yards away, under a full head of steam. I reached for the phone and called the superintendent, explaining to the secretary that she, the superintendent, may want to talk to me ASAP. Knowledge is power; my superintendent backed me up and was grateful for not being blindsided.

If you expect to develop trust with your superintendent and the central office, you must keep them informed about anything that may reach them. The superintendent will not look at you as incompetent if you tell him or her of problems on the way. In fact, you will find yourself in serious trouble if a problem gets to the superintendent as a surprise and you knew it was coming.

I always send memos or make phone calls to prepare the central office for a problem on the way. Asking for help on problems with school management or budget will be welcome as long as they are real concerns and not items you should handle yourself. *My rule is, if it could involve the central office, ask and inform.*

COMMUNICATING WITH THE COMMUNITY OUTSIDE THE SCHOOL

You can shoot yourself in the foot if you fail to keep the community informed and involved in your school. The best way to stay out of trouble is to not have secrets. Secrets lead to rumors, and rumors unchecked can get you fired.

Newsletter. Newsletters were my primary method of informing the public. These were mailed to the home of the student, not carried home by the student. I wanted to make sure the newsletters arrived at the home, so we purchased a bulk mail permit and used it often. The newsletter was simple to do. There were regular columns from the Principal, the Student Activities Director, the Counselor, and the Home and School Club. Each newsletter included a calendar for the balance of the year, with details for the current month and any announcements that I wanted to communicate. A secretary did the typing, but I encouraged the contributors to come to the secretary's computer and enter their column themselves. (This is easily done just by bringing a disk with the column saved on it and entering it into the newsletter template.) A regular deadline was maintained, and the secretary in charge was responsible for reminding everyone to get his or her part in on time. The letter was printed in the office, folded, labeled, and taken to the post office by volunteer parents.

Home and School Club. The Home and School (H&S) Club, known as the PTA in some schools, offers a face-to-face contact with the community. At my school the officers of the H&S Club were also the officers of the site council. This was extremely convenient for communication between the two, and since the meetings of both organizations were held back to back on the same night it cut down on meeting nights for me. The H&S Club raised money to support classroom teachers and other activities on the campus. I *always* started the meeting with a 15- to 20-minute overview of what was going on on the campus. I always did my homework and presented a professional and positive posture. This feature alone was so popular that it virtually guaranteed that no one was late. My report covered many things in the newsletter but also such things as "why you saw a police car here on Wednesday" or "you may have heard the rumor of a fight on Tuesday." This time allowed me to have the attention of the group to explain my reasons for decisions, such as not allowing limousines at a school dance; my personal philosophy; or how we as a staff resolved to do something.

Site Council. The site council is a formal organization in California. It has the responsibility to spend money for school improvement that is received from the state. So that no one group can dominate, the rules state that the council must be composed of 50%

community members and 50% staff. Officers and members are elected and by agreement from the Home and School Club the officers elected served as officers in both organizations. Since both had money to spend, this guaranteed that money would be spent efficiently and without conflict. Our meetings often had many more in attendance at the site council meetings than official members. Everyone had the right to contribute and participate in discussion. Decisions were by consensus with the agreement that if there was a disagreement between elected members we would call for an official vote from just the elected members. We never had to call for an official vote in 7 years because we never had an impasse.

Web Page/E-Mail. I was not principal during a time when electronic technology was as common as today. If I were a principal now, I would make sure that I had a school web page that was updated regularly (weekly) and an e-mail newsletter to parents and students who wished to be on the list. I would also have e-mail surveys and links to me. One caution—remember that a major part of your community does not have the ability to connect to your system for the web page or e-mail. This means that the information you receive will not represent those people. From Owatonna Jr. High School in Owatonna, Minnesota, Bill Sommers, who is the principal there, reports that his school was constructing a web page complete with school calendar, assignments, and upcoming events. The page was very popular, with many hits a day.

Phone Message Machine. Many schools have a phone line dedicated to a message machine. The machine is programmed daily to provide anyone who calls with information about the school and its activities. Some schools use a similar process for a homework hot line. I specifically chose not to do that for one reason. I wanted the students to develop responsibility for recording their own homework or phoning a friend when they were absent or missed something. Thus they could develop a lifelong habit that leads to responsibility, something we should be teaching.

People Who Talk. One idea that came from a superintendent I worked for, John Prieskorn, is a jewel. As you move about the community, begin to build a file of names, phone numbers, and addresses of people who talk to people on a regular basis. These are the barbers and hairdressers, market and bank clerks, postal employees and businesspeople who are out there and talking. These people then can become the target of accurate information about your school and how it is doing educating students. Make sure that these people receive every announcement and letter and visit them when you can to personally make sure that they get the story straight from "the horse's mouth." This can be your number one way to keep deadly rumors at bay and make sure that you get your story out the way you want it to be heard.

Newspapers. Educators do not pay close attention to public relations issues. We often complain about how the newspaper "got it wrong again!" as we read yet another article condemning education, and we often exhibit impotence by blaming our problems on other people. John Prieskorn again had the right idea to take control of a story. His method is threefold: (a) write your own column, (b) write the reporters' columns, and (c) call the papers before they call you. If you have the time, writing a column in a local paper allows you to reach a large population with the story you want people to hear. I also wrote press releases in a format that reporters could submit with their byline, thus saving them time and again getting my story out. Finally, calling the papers when something happens or when I wanted to get noticed for something allows me to talk to them on my time. Even if they only get it 80% correct, that is still a B and keeps public opinion going your way.

Four-Foot Mail Carriers. As a last resort I would send material home with students. This process works best with younger children and begins to fall off in reliability in middle and high school. All you have to do is look around the campus to see if your notices are getting home, especially if they are printed on brightly colored paper. A contest with something for the class that gets every parent to respond to something sent home helps with reliability, but I recommend staying away from this method if you want to be sure the parents have a chance to see the message. Also remember that this method only reaches parents in the community and not the other members who should also know what their tax money is accomplishing.

Direct Mail. What else is there to say? If you want to be sure that it gets there, mail it. Bulk mail is cheap and only needs to be bundled correctly. Student clubs can help in folding, stuffing, labeling, and sorting.

WHERE DO IDEAS COME FROM— BOTTOM UP OR TOP DOWN?

One of the greatest surprises to me when I first became a principal was that during brainstorming sessions with staff members they would think that everything I talked about was something I wanted to do. They would rush around attempting to implement my ideas or start complaining, "There he goes again, expecting miracles."

The problem exists around the question, "Where do ideas come from, bottom up or top down?" The answer is, "Yes! Bottom up *and* top down."

The principal is at one time a leader and a colleague. A good principal attempts to remain a colleague in many areas. One of these areas is as an advocate for students and improving student learning. This the principal can do by engaging in and encouraging discussion before decisions are made—offering and accepting ideas, debating and refining concepts, assisting in decision making or making decisions himself or herself. It is the last, making decisions alone, that leads to the feeling among staff that everything the principal does is top down. It is important that the principal is clear about when he or she is or is not making a top-down decision.

This idea first hit me at a faculty meeting. I stopped what we were doing and said, "I want to make things clear. I have been a teacher for over 20 years and a principal for over 3. Just because I say something does not mean I am making a final decision. I have a right to make suggestions, just as you do, as part of this school community. I will be very clear when it is a suggestion and when it is an order from now on."

From that moment on I would always start out a discussion with the words, "This is an item for discussion. We are brainstorming and debating." I would usually try to sit down with the staff at that time, and not stand so that I could avoid maintaining the focus as an authority figure.

On the other hand, if I was making a final decision or offering something that could not be debated at the time I would state, "I need to let you know that this is a decision I am making." Or I might say, "Thank you for your suggestions, but I am making this next decision and here is what it is."

Most decisions can be made by discussion and consensus.

Faculty Meetings   Box 1.3

Sitting in the sweltering heat of a September day in Felton, California, with 30 other teachers, I saw the stare of hate directed at one of my colleagues. He had been reading the newspaper and something from the discussion had penetrated his occupied mind at the end of a long, long faculty meeting. Aroused from his self-induced stupor, he chose to ask a "clarifying" question. It didn't matter that we had been discussing the very point he was questioning for the last hour, it didn't matter that we had answered his question many times over, it didn't matter that he looked stupid, he asked it anyway, and the principal, seemingly unaware that it was 5:40 PM and the meeting was supposed to have been over at 4:00 PM, obliviously began a long explanation, again. After all, it was his meeting, not ours. Teachers groaned; the teacher's friends kicked at his feet and made faces. Someone said, "Where have you been?" Very few ever paid attention at these meetings—they graded papers, stared blankly into space, knitted, read newspapers, read books, doodled on papers, or talked quietly to each other. All the time, the principal droned on and on. I swore at that time that if I ever became a principal I would rather die than have meaningless meetings and waste the staff's time. Time is our most precious nonrenewable resource!

Most of you recognize the story. At faculty meetings, teachers often behave in ways that they would never allow students in their own classes to behave, and principals allow them to do it. You know, you have all been there. What is wrong with this picture? I endured 21 years of faculty meeting as a teacher and cannot remember one good meeting. I do remember meetings that were scheduled to be out at 4:00 PM going on until 5:30! I do remember thinking, "Just shut up!" Or, "I will kill the next person who asks a question!" And, "Why doesn't he put this stuff in a memo?" I also remember thinking that if I ever became a principal I would not do things this way.

As a principal, I experimented with different formats and arrived at the following based upon the notion that meetings are for communication and decision making.

Faculty Meetings

1. I established the following meeting monthly schedule

> The first Wednesday—3:00 PM to 4:00 PM—All-Faculty Business Meeting: At this meeting we received information that could not be communicated by memo, clarified memo communications, made group decisions, and covered any other business information.

> Second Wednesday—3:00 PM to 4:00 PM—Principal's Cabinet (eight members): Similar to a department chairpersons meeting, this group was my main teacher advisory council and communication route to the various disciplines in the school.

> Third Wednesday—3:00 PM to 4:30 PM—All-Faculty Staff Development Meeting: This was a time for all of us to learn together.

> Fourth Wednesday—3:00 PM to 4:00 PM—Department Meetings: At this time the representatives to the Principal's Cabinet conducted department business meetings.

2. I made a promise that all meetings would last until the agenda was covered or the time for the meeting expired, *whichever came first*, if the staff would
    a. Read all memos as they were distributed.
    b. Arrive at the meeting on time.
    c. Be present and attentive throughout the meeting; this meant *no* other activities, that is, reading, knitting, grading papers, and so on, during the meeting. This was important because time is lost when people are not paying attention and have to ask clarifying questions.

3. I started all meetings precisely on time so that those who were there on time did not have to waste time and so that those who chose

to be late could see that I would not keep others waiting for them. I enforced the rules and I placed a note in the mailbox of those entering a meeting late urging them to be on time in the future, in a polite way at first, but then personally talked to them if they persisted. During the meeting I would remind people who were working on other things to please put them away.

My motto in all of this was, "I will not waste your time; please don't waste mine." It was not long before the staff took the rules for granted and I no longer had to "ride herd" on them.

FACULTY MEETING—BUSINESS

On the back of the door to my office, I installed two hooks that held a chart paper pack. This was not only convenient to use during meetings in my office but served as my agenda builder for meetings. On it I would "mind-map" the agenda for faculty business meetings. The map consisted of the meeting date in a circle in the center of the

Figure 1.1. Agenda Map

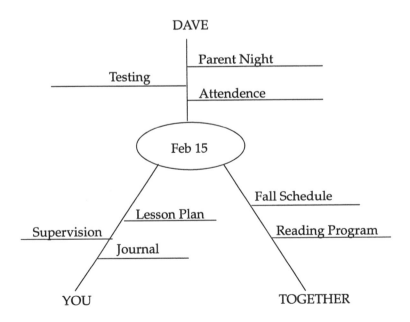

page with three long lines radiating outward toward the edges of the paper, dividing it into thirds (see Figure 1.1). One line was labeled "Dave," the next "Together," and the third "You." This chart was available on the door for the entire month. As items came to mind or were turned in to my secretary, I would add them to the diagram as herringbone branches. On the "Dave" line I wrote announcements and items that would not require discussion. The "Together" line had items that required discussion and input from the entire group, and the "You" line referred to business that was up to each individual teacher to work on alone. This line also included journal prompts for reflection outlined (journals will be discussed in a later chapter).

I would chair the meeting and use a red felt pen to check off each item as we covered it. Discussions were carefully orchestrated. I always had the staff consider discussion items in their journals before talking about them. This act alone raised the level of response to higher orders and more complete thoughts. I also called on people to speak. Once a person spoke to an issue, that person could not speak again until all the staff members had the opportunity to speak; then the person could speak again. Eventually, I would cut off the discussion, and we would arrive at consensus if consensus were appropriate. Other times, I would announce my decision. Consensus was achieved by asking if there was anyone who could not live with the decision. If someone had a concern, I asked the person to make the change in the wording that would make it OK and then asked the question again. This we repeated until there were no major concerns.

When time was up, the meeting adjourned. We rarely had to go over time. Because I asked the staff to write and reflect, their input was thoughtful and difficult-to-follow thinking out loud was avoided. As a result, we saved time during the meeting and completed more work.

Another advantage of the deep thinking process I encouraged was that our decisions were more thoroughly thought out. These decisions rarely had to be revisited, thus saving more time.

The purpose of the Principal's Cabinet was to allow communication and discussion in a casual atmosphere with a smaller group. Any department representative could add an item to the agenda. There were no "off limits" items. One of the other duties of these elected representatives was to evaluate the principal twice a year. I would ask them to go out to their departments and make the following statement:

> It is time to let the principal know what he is doing well and where he needs to improve. He is neither all good nor all bad. This is not a complaint session. If you have something good to say, you must provide evidence. If you have a "needs to improve" statement, you must provide the incident and provide a statement of how it could be done differently.

The department would talk it over at a department meeting, and the representatives would bring the results to the next cabinet meeting.

At that meeting I would sit as part of the circle—we always met in a circle—and each department representative would tell me the results of that department's meeting while I took notes. I would always respond, often in agreement of the needs to improve, and explain if the change requested was illegal or too expensive. I found that all the observations were reasonable. I would then report out the results at the next Faculty Business Meeting. I believe that you cannot credibly evaluate others if you do not allow your colleagues to evaluate you. This process also allowed me to grow professionally.

When he was the assistant principal at Wayzata High School, Bill Sommers started having departments host faculty meetings. The departments would plan refreshments and presentations to increase common knowledge about the curriculum and the various ideas they were introducing into their programs.

STUDENT AND TEACHER HANDBOOKS

As soon as you can, preferably before the teachers and students return for your first full year, you should rewrite and reorganize the student and teacher handbooks. These are the first products that the teachers and public can see each year that conveys your philosophy and leadership style.

As an example, I belonged to the Josephson Institute of Ethics. This group publishes a small card with the "Six Pillars of Character" and "Doing the Right Thing, Making Ethical Choices based on the

Six Pillars of Character." These guidelines are so important to me that I included them in the handbooks for both students and teachers. Many parents commented on them and expressed their support for that philosophy. It is one of the few things that I never received a negative comment about.

MAKING EXECUTIVE DECISIONS

Although I like a shared decision making process for most decisions, there are times where the principal does not have time to get input and must make the decision himself or herself. The principal must be careful—or risk the destruction of trust if he or she is not tactful. An example is the editing of the teacher and student handbooks during the summer before you take over. This is a time when most teachers are not available to consult with. You may find items in the existing manuals that you must change because they do not fit your philosophy. You must make the changes immediately because if you do not you will end up having to defend some rule or regulation that you absolutely cannot support. Make sure that these autocratic moves are only on items you absolutely cannot live with. Further changes can be made with staff input for the next editions.

While reading the student handbook, I came across two rules for which I absolutely could find no professional reason. The first was the rule, "Pencils are not allowed for anything except math." This bothered me, since most students did not have word processors at that time, and many still do not. So what is wrong with pencils on rough drafts and papers where corrections may have to be made? Pencils are user friendly. I understand that students should learn the need to use ink on a formal paper, but on any other paper what is wrong with pencil? Thoreau wrote almost exclusively with pencils, and I do not think it hurt him professionally. Thomas Edison had pencils made especially to fit in his vest pockets because they were his preferred writing instruments. So I took the rule out.

The other similar rule was, "All students will use cursive writing on all papers." Why? What is the reason to make it a rule? I know that cursive is faster, but is it not up to the user which way he or she prefers to write? I do not know of any forms that say, "Please use cursive." In fact, some people, young boys especially, have small motor problems, and printing is easier for them. If the purpose of writing is to communicate, who cares whether or not a person prints or uses cursive? So I took that rule out.

If you are going to change rules, remember to highlight them to the staff so that they know about the change. Also remember that there are rules that were made for some reason locally, so you could step on toes if you are not careful. Be sure to communicate changes to the staff if you do make changes without their input.

Communication is the start of it all. Administrators cannot expect results if they cannot communicate what they want and how they want it done and do it in a way that encourages others to listen and act. Trust is only built through open and truthful communication; it is a two-way process. Administrators not only need to convey their message; they also need to listen to what others are saying to them and be clear in what they expect from the school community.

NOTE

1. Throughout the book, I/me refers to David R. Schumaker. Coauthor William A. Sommers is referred to as Bill Sommers or Bill.

2

Trusting Yourself, Trusting Others

She knocked on my door with an urgency that demanded my attention. I said, "Come in." The door opened and in stomped one of my best, one of my most trusted teachers, and one of the few with whom I was able to share my confidential thoughts without fear of a leak. She was also a person I would never suspect of believing in rumors, let alone preposterous ones. Yet there she was, glaring at me. I asked her to sit down. "I can see that you are upset. What seems to be the problem?"

She blurted out, "I understand that the textbook companies have sent you sets of sample history books and that you have them hidden in the district office because you don't want us to spend the money on new books!"

The rumor was not true but my concern was real. Trust is ethereal and you can never take it for granted. It is a two-part word: trusting and trustworthy. Both are absolutely necessary if you are going to be an effective principal. In the beginning people are willing to grant you the benefit of the doubt and award you a tentative trust. As time goes by they will test and observe you, holding you accountable for what you say and do. If you pass the test the level of trust will go up and up. The problem is, no matter how long you are trusted and no matter how high the trust level is, if you drop your guard and betray people's trust just once the level of trust will plunge to zero and stay there for a time. You can regain some of the trust granted to you, but it will never return to the high level you had before the fall.

People are forgiving about many things, but not about trust. You are the boss and you are in a position to cause trouble for the people who work for you. This means that there is always an undercurrent of suspicion about anything you do. Many people will automatically look for the "real" reason you are doing things. So it is important that you are careful about what you say and do.

GOODWILL BANK

Gayle Carino, one of my teachers, once told me a story about an incident with her father when she was a teenager. It seems that one evening she asked her father if she could use the family car to go out with some friends. She expected that he would just give her the keys, since it was obvious that the car was not in use. Instead he asked her if she had made any deposits in the goodwill bank, because she was asking to make a withdrawal.

That metaphor struck me, since it came at a time when students were being treated like second-class citizens, by the staff, and the staff was not happy with the past administration.

As administrators, we are forever requesting withdrawals. Could you supervise this extra event? We need volunteers for . . . I know you have had a full day but . . . Please get to class. Pick up your trash. What do we do to make deposits?

After thinking about the story, I made the goodwill bank a part of my vocabulary and a passion. It was a matter of trust.

I started with the office. We made an effort to treat everyone who entered with respect until he or she earned our disrespect. Students were greeted the same way as adults. At passing times I always said please and thank you when asking and getting cooperation. I helped students in and out of doors. I gave them my time and energy in a happy and joyous way. When I found teachers not behaving that way, I would talk to them privately. I would tell them Gayle's story and ask them to please make the goodwill bank deposits, because someday we would have to make withdrawals.

That time came, more than once. One time in particular was on the day that the Persian Gulf War started. My school was in a liberal town with a university nearby. Many of the students' parents had been involved with antiwar protests in the past, and the students felt that it was time for them to protest. The only problem was, they were not sure how.

As they milled around looking for a way to demonstrate, several teachers taught them the song "We Shall Overcome" and stood in a circle with the students holding hands and singing. It was lunchtime and you could feel the excitement in the air. The end of lunch bell rang and the students made no effort to go back to class. I let the protest go for about 20 more minutes and then asked the teachers who were out in the yard helping to supervise the students to go open their rooms and on the way gently tell the students that it was time to return to class where they could talk more about the war. I reminded them that we had been making many deposits in the goodwill bank and it was time to see if we could make a withdrawal.

The teachers opened the rooms while the vice principal, counselor, teachers on prep period, and I moved among the students saying, "I know it is a serious time and you are very worried about the war, however, I need for you to go back to class now, where you can talk with your teachers about the war. Thank you." We were making a request. It was not an order, and the students knew and felt that they were being treated in a different way from what they had expected.

Within 5 or 10 minutes the campus was clear of all but seven students who refused to return to their classrooms. I merely called their parents and requested that they come get their children. The crisis passed. I immediately went to the speaker system, a system that I only use at the beginning or end of the day unless there is an emergency or something extremely important that can't wait, and made the following announcement:

"I wish to thank each and every student for returning to your classroom when I requested you to do so. I know that these are difficult and exciting times—many of you have friends and relatives involved in a dangerous war and are rightfully concerned. You behaved like adults at this time, and I am proud of you all."

We had made the withdrawal, and I was immediately beginning to make new deposits. The behavior of our students was in sharp contrast to the other schools in the area, where many students marched across town and caused a dangerous disruption of traffic and school time.

Teachers too need deposits. Discussion of one such area follows.

TREATING ADULT PROFESSIONALS
AS ADULT PROFESSIONALS

When I first became a principal, I was always surprised what an adult professional will ask my permission to do. For example,

- ◆ If I get someone to cover my last class, will you let me go to the dentist?
- ◆ My wife has to leave on a business trip tomorrow and I have to get the kids off to school. I may be a few minutes late, is that OK? (We had a district policy that all teachers would be in their rooms 30 minutes before school started with the doors open.)
- ◆ I feel sick and need to go lie down. Is it OK if someone covers my class?

The requests go on and on. These are from people we trust with our future leaders and we treat them like the children in our schools. We often defend our actions on the grounds of some behaviors of the worst of us. Sure, we are taken advantage of from time to time. Sure, there are teachers and other staff members who do not deserve our respect and trust, but they are in the minority. I do not know many of my colleagues who cannot be trusted to do the right thing.

My stated policy in this situation was, "You are adult professionals, and until I have a reason to believe differently I will treat you as such." If you have need to leave early or arrive late or if you have to be out of your class for any reason you feel is a professional need, just make sure your students are supervised by a credentialed person, let me know who is covering, and go.

This act alone made huge deposits in the goodwill bank. I was rarely disappointed, and on that rare occasion I went to the person who had violated my trust personally and did not punish the entire staff.

Any system has a culture that can be sensed by strangers entering it. When you enter a Neiman-Marcus store, it is evident to most people that this is a store that is a cut above the others. You do not have to be told. The same is true of a school. As a result of our effort at goodwill, we often heard that a visitor could feel the difference from the moment he or she walked onto the campus. The Program

Quality Review Team wrote in its final report, "It was apparent that something good was happening with kids on this campus. We felt it the moment we stepped onto the campus and it continued throughout the day. Students consistently let us know that they were happy and felt appreciated." I feel we owe that, in part, to the attention we paid to the goodwill of our students.

At Owatonna Jr. High School, the staff was the recipient of proceeds from the goodwill bank through the "One Hour Sabbatical" program. Bill Sommers and his assistant principal hand a coupon to a teacher every time they catch one in the hallway greeting students during passing time. On Thursday, popcorn day for the teachers, while the teachers are taking a break and eating popcorn all the coupons are placed in a box and a name drawn. That teacher wins a one-hour sabbatical on any day the next week. The principal or vice principal substitutes for the teacher during the hour.

In the above case, both teachers and students are recipients of goodwill.

MAKING PEOPLE PART OF THE PROCESS

The main function of a school is to educate students. No school can truly function well unless *all* participants consider themselves part of the process of education. "All" means parents, teachers, aides, students, counselors, classified staff, and administrators. This makes the job of principal a true balancing act. If people are to truly feel that they are part of the educational process, then they must truly be part of the process and not given just a token role. The process of involving has three parts in my view. These are, in the order of increasing responsibility, *advisory, shared decision making,* and *shared leadership*. No matter which process you involve people in, you must make it clear which role the people will play and how their input will be used.

Advisory

The advisory role is just that. Questions are brought to advisory groups or people to obtain advice that will lead to a decision in the long run. Examples are the Home and School Club, individuals, business groups, student council, clubs, and focus parent groups. "Focus parent groups" is a term I use for those groups of parents that form around a single concern such as homework policy, discipline, or graduation requirements. These groups of people are consulted whenever a decision that will affect their concern is addressed. This does not mean that they have the power to force their way, but they must be consulted in a sincere way and their opinions taken seriously. I use the Home and School Club, similar to a PTA, regularly for this purpose. I introduce a topic and usually use a chart pack with bold felt pens to record the advice for all to see. Then these pieces of information are typed up and included in the minutes. When a decision is finally made, I make it a point to tell the group how its input influenced the final decision.

Student groups, such as the student council, clubs, or teams, are treated the same way. When I first became a middle school principal, I asked all the sports team members what they felt that they needed most at the school. I learned that a new track was high on the list of almost everyone. The school was in an area with a Mediterranean climate and wet all winter. The students, teams and PE alike, wanted an all-weather track to run on. I communicated this to the superintendent and other groups interested in the school, and within a year we had a donated quarter-mile track with an all-weather surface. I let the students and teachers know that it was partly due to their influence that this was accomplished.

Shared Decision Making

The process of shared decision making is a step up on the responsibility scale. The groups and individuals generally given this responsibility are the vice principal, counselors, site councils, and the school staff (clerical staff, maintenance workers, grounds workers, and faculty). They are encouraged to share in the decision-making process with the principal. Here again the people consulted must understand their role in the process. I make it clear that I am giving them the responsibility to make decisions with my input and that there may be a time when a decision made is one that I cannot support.

When I cannot support a decision, I make it clear what the problem is, and then we work it out from there. Most of the time, however, these groups make very wise decisions if they have all the information needed for good decisions.

The process of shared decision making starts with informing the decision makers about all parts of the question. For instance, when I was considering changing the eighth grade from a traditional departmentalized language arts and social studies program to a more integrated core structure, I started by providing all the staff, not just those involved, with background articles and discussions about the benefits and pitfalls of changing or staying the same. I sent teachers out to schools that had eighth-grade core programs. We held discussions, and at first there was major resistance against the change from the eighth-grade language arts and social studies teachers. This was to be expected. I needed to keep in mind that people often resist change even if it appears to be for the best. Also, I had to keep in mind that people would return to old habits if the change was not in place long enough to really test it. The basic rule was, once a decision was made it would be in place for a predetermined period of time. At the end of the predetermined time period, the decision was reviewed by those involved, adjustments were made if needed, and then it was tested for another predetermined period of time. In this case the change would be for one year; then we would review, adjust, and test for another year, a spiral feedback process. See Chapter 3, "Learning to Change (and Liking It)" for a more complete explanation of this example.

Another consideration when making these decisions is how to provide support to the people participating in the change. I can remember Dick Patterson, my first superintendent in the Soquel Elementary School District in California, where I was principal, telling me, "Dave, by September of next year you will have a bilingual program for Grades 6 to 8 in place. Now, your responsibility is to tell us"—pointing to himself and the other administrators at the meeting—"how we can help you do this." I had a very small Spanish-speaking-only population at the middle school and not enough to warrant programs at each grade level. I called together my bilingual people and had them put their heads together to design a solution. They came up with a core 6-7-8 combined bilingual multiperiod program. The solution worked well, and by the fall we had the teacher-designed program in place.

Another example was my special education program. My problem was that students in special education pull-out programs often suffer from low self-esteem because they are singled out in pull-out programs with special teachers. The fact that they are not in the mainstream of the school leaves many of them feeling left out. I told the prospective seventh- and eighth-grade mainstream special education core teachers I would help them get training, secure materials, and develop programs. I also told them that if we could mainstream those students, they could also be assisted by the special education teachers on a daily basis, since those teachers would no longer have the responsibility of the pull-out program. I also told them that if they worked at the program for one year they could opt out the next year if they wished.

The teachers volunteered and began immediately to work together to design an effective program. The program's basic design included two special education mainstream cores at Grades 7 and 8. A full-time teacher and a part-time special education teacher staffed each core. Furthermore, the special education students would have special passes to a special education tutor who would also help other students in the school when not working with the special education students, making full use of the tutor's time. All special education students were programmed into one of these cores, many of them without knowing that they were identified. The program was a smashing success, with enthusiastic parent support because the students' needs were attended to at the same time the chosen students were feeling a part of the school again. As a final bonus, all of the teachers in the first-year program elected to stay with it the next two years.

At a nearby high school, there was a different story of how a poor approach to decision making led to discontent. A decision to go to block scheduling was made by the administration, and the teachers were told that it would be better for them as teachers. No consideration was given to student achievement. The teachers did not truly participate in the decision. It was made, and they were led to believe that it was the teachers' choice.

One day I received a call from a friend in the district. He asked, "What are some other block schedules for us to consider? Many of the teachers don't like the one we are on and we want to change." My answer was, "How are the students doing with the block schedule? Why did you go to a block schedule anyway?" He thought for a moment and responded, "I can see that we have a lot to do before we pursue this change." He told me that he would approach the principal with the idea of assessing the present program and how well the students were learning on the present schedule.

Another example came during the summer of 1996, when California Governor Pete Wilson mandated class size reduction for Grades K through 3. There was no warning, and there seemed to be no teacher participation in the decision. Districts were not expecting it as their schools let out for the summer. The fall hiring was almost completed when suddenly the decision was announced. The reduction for Grades K through 2 had to be completed as schools opened in September. New teachers had to be hired. The substitute rolls were decimated as they were scoured for warm bodies to use as teachers. Many poorly qualified teachers were swept into the classroom, often without credentials. To accommodate new staff, classroom space had to be created and furniture, books, and supplies purchased. The companies that made portable rooms were swamped with orders and could not fill them. The problem was so immense that by September many students found themselves packed into a classroom with two teachers and two classes. Sharing books was not unusual. Teachers were not prepared to work with the smaller class size. Most continued to use methods they had learned while teaching larger classes and lacked the training to maximize the benefit of the smaller classes to students.

Major conflicts developed as the districts with higher teacher salaries hired seasoned veterans, often the best, from less wealthy districts, leaving those districts with the bulk of the poorer teachers. At the same time, teachers in Grades 4 to 5 or 6 in the same schools were expected to teach as large or larger classes to accommodate the change, which left them angry with the system. The lower-grade teachers were often floundering and frustrated. This became a perfect example of what happens when a top-down decision is forced on a system without adequate time to plan for the change. For years, educators have been asking for smaller class sizes. Suddenly we have it, and now elementary schools are being evaluated. It is expected by the politicians and parents that all student learning in the lower grades will go up. If it does not, the case can be made by the media and politicians that, "we gave them what they wanted and it didn't do any good." All because the process was top down without proper preparation for instituting a good idea.

Staff members will do as they are told, to a certain degree, but will do so grudgingly. On the other hand, staff members will throw all of their creative energy into defining, refining, and implementing a decision that they have been involved with. Most teachers want to be considered professionals and demonstrate that when they are involved decisions are more effective and more globally received.

Shared Leadership

Shared leadership is the highest level of sharing in the decision process. In the process of shared leadership, an individual or group other than the principal is given the authority to make a decision without the involvement of the principal. A principal, or a superintendent for that matter, cannot do everything or be everywhere and therefore needs help with the work. The person or group given the responsibility for a decision must understand the rules. They must keep in mind that a principal cannot support something that goes against his or her philosophy or vision and cannot condone a decision that is against policy or the law.

The principal must also understand when granting a shared leadership role to another party that the decision may or may not be exactly what he or she would have hoped for or expected. The principal must determine the answer to the question, "Can I live with this decision?" If not, the principal has a very difficult problem. That problem is how to get the decision altered to one he or she can support without alienating the people involved.

To avoid this problem, the principal must be careful to choose people to be involved with shared leadership who share the same vision for the school.

RELATIONSHIPS—STUDENTS, PARENTS, NEIGHBORHOOD, BUSINESS PARTNERSHIPS, MEDIA

Public education is not good at public relations. Look at any major corporation and you will find a large portion of money spent on developing ways to make the company look good to the public. It is a trust-building activity, and if done well it pays off with a better public understanding of our job and how well we do it. If public relations work is done poorly or not at all, educators deserve what they get. If we continue to let other people tell us how we are doing, then how can we expect to have our story accurately told?

The basics of trust building involve being aware of everyone in your sphere of influence. You cannot leave anyone or any group out if you want to be successful. Starting with students, the idea of building trust should be foremost in your mind every waking moment. Never promise anything you cannot deliver. Never talk about confidential items with anyone who does not need to know. Always deliver when you say you will. Keep people informed. Tell the truth, always.

I clearly remember an incident while I was still teaching high school. I was out for an off-campus lunchtime walk and came on the beginning of a fight between two boys. A large audience of boys surrounded the two protagonists who were facing off in the center. Words were flying and fists were cocked and ready to fly. As I squeezed my way into the center of the group, I was thinking that each boy had everything to lose by backing down in front of such a large crowd. I was the only adult in a group of forty 17- and 18-year-old young men.

As I reached the center I stepped between the two boys and said, "What's going on, guys? I would like to ask you to come with me." My idea was to get them away from the group first.

"Hell no!" was the answer from one boy, who went on to say that he could not afford to be taken to the principal.

I responded by saying that I only wanted to talk to them and that if they had not been fighting I would not take them to the principal—I only wanted to talk. I did not know either boy. They both looked at me with doubt, even hate, and I was very worried that I would be involved if they decided to swing.

One boy said, "I don't believe you."

From the crowd of onlookers I heard a voice yell, "You can trust him, he's cool." With that I asked the crowd to go back to campus. One by one they began to leave, and the two potential fighters stayed.

When we were alone, I asked the two boys to come with me to my room on the campus. They walked with me in between and the two arguing with each other across me.

We sat in my room for some time talking. I got a promise of no fight and had one of them come see me after school. There was no fight.

This is known as the "Gunsmoke Technique." Each side involved in the face-off really does not want to fight. They were hoping for Marshal Dillon to break it up.

It never could have happened if there had been no trust. Of course, if the fight had started or if it had taken place later, I would have turned them in to the principal. They knew that. They knew that I was not their "friend." I was, however, a friendly adult who had responsibilities to the system but could be trusted with my word.

I have to warn the reader that we live in a different world today. Walking into a fight can be very dangerous. The story is used only to illustrate the point of trust and the goodwill bank and not to advocate attempting to stop a fight single-handedly.

Within the first month that I started as principal of New Brighton Middle School, I began to walk the neighborhood at various times of the day. I knocked at doors and talked to people, introducing myself, asking their concerns, giving them my card and asking them to call me with any concerns or information. I told them to tell my secretary that they were school neighbors and that would give them a quick path to me. From that process I received calls about good and bad things going on. People told me of fights starting, vandalism, and kids who treated them well. One caller expressed concerns for the students' hearing, stating that during a dance she could hear the music a block away. In every case, I followed up and then called the person back to report on the results.

The media are another area where trust goes a long way. How often do we complain about how education is "treated" in the media? There is hardly a day that goes by without some negative press. "Dream Team High School graduate arrested as mass murderer!" shouts at us from the headlines. The fact that the accused graduated 20 years ago is rarely noted in the headline. No headline screams, "Harmony Church attendee arrested in sex scandal." Schools take the brunt of political and public criticism, and people always seem ready to believe the worst about us.

We cannot do much about the sensational headlines, but we can have a major effect on how the local media treat us. I learned this from a former superintendent of mine, John Prieskorn. He told me to make a connection with the media and involve them in the school. Write articles for the paper that can be sent to reporters with a note that they can put their own byline on it if they wish. Educational reporters are always behind the eight ball for time and copy. Your generosity will pay off in the long run.

When I became a principal I began to cultivate the local reporter who was assigned the education beat for a city newspaper as well as the local editor. No matter what was happening, I would call the newspaper reporter to let her know my thoughts. This would give me the first shot at telling my view of the situation. As the article developed, she would often call me back to ask questions and that gave me another shot at the story. Finally, when the article ran, I would usually discover that it was mostly correct in my view—usually 90% correct, which is not bad and is usually considered an A in any grading system. I learned to look at the article for its overall effect and quality, and if it was generally positive and correct I would call the reporter to thank her for her good reporting. The same was true for a local editor. I purchased him a copy of the book *The Manufactured Crisis* (Berliner & Biddle, 1995) and asked him to read it and then to meet with me. The book is about how the constant negative reporting of how America's schools are doing is greatly distorted for political reasons. The book shows how we are really doing as educators and how to read testing results in a more objective way.

Remember, however, my favorite phrase in this situation, "We are neither all good nor all bad." Do not defend the indefensible. There are usually many areas where we are sorely lacking and others where we are doing well. If you expect to be trusted and to have a positive effect on the media, you must be honest and truthful about what you support or attack.

Local business can be a great partner and offer you another opportunity to get objective feedback as well as have input into opinions about public education. In my community, we are encouraged to make partnerships with local businesses. In most of my experience, the first reason that schools think a business partnership will be good for them is for what they can "get" from the business. This thought usually is for money or equipment, and although it is nice if it happens I feel that it is not the first reason we should partner with a business.

I prefer to partner with a small business for several reasons. Most of our students will work for small businesses, and a small business usually has more contact with the community the school serves. I want a partnership to be a two-way pairing where the school and the business learn from each other.

One partnership we had was with a local company that manufactured beachwear. They wanted to partner with our school to help students learn about what it takes to keep a job in a small business and highlight that students could not count on making a living surfing in the ocean.

Although the partnership ended when the management focus changed, we were on our way to several benefits for both parties. Among those that the company gained were feedback on clothing designs from young people, volunteers for community projects such as a local surfing contest, and a ready audience for champion surfers to tell about the facts of their work world. We were to receive help with our yearbook from the company's graphic arts department, a surfing machine for our PE program, and some summer employment for our students as well as local heroes telling our students to stay in school. Some of the agreement was completed before the change and a parting of the ways, but I found that the company still spoke highly of us at local Rotary and Chamber of Commerce meetings.

Speaking about education issues at public meetings became a quest for me. I put together three talks of approximately 30 minutes that I could give in a lively manner to community clubs and organizations. I usually gave three or four a year and the returns were outstanding. I made connections through these efforts and others that allowed me to call on local businesses for help when I needed it. As an example, when I needed to move 500 chairs from storage across town to our gym for graduation, a local department store and moving company provided trucks and personnel for the job. I published thanks in the newspaper for all to read.

HAVING FUN TOGETHER

All work and no play certainly makes a job more difficult, if not impossible. The work of teachers is stressful at best and physically damaging at worst. I have heard that the job of teacher is second in stress only to that of an air traffic controller, with physical manifestations such as early tooth decay, bladder infections, hypertension, and mental problems. One way to alleviate some of the stress is to have fun when you can as a staff.

One of my first acts was to start the Sunshine and Morale, or SAM Club. All of the teachers at New Brighton Middle School

(NBMS) had to sign up for a prescribed number of adjunct duties. I called in two of the most creative people I knew and made the proposal that if they would find ways for the staff to have fun together they would not have any adjunct duties. NBMS already had Friday treats in the morning. Friday treats was an institution where a pair of staff members would bring treats every Friday morning. It was a rotating assignment and ranged from bagels and various spreads to full breakfasts cooked on Coleman stoves. Usually the snacks increased in elegance as the weeks progressed until finally someone would reach the top with something delicious and elaborate. If the next person in line attempted to top it, he or she would face financial ruin. At that point the next snack was usually back to basics, bagels and spreads.

The SAM team took to the work with enthusiasm and energy. Members sent out surveys to other schools, asking them for ideas for having fun and promising to share the ideas. From this we had a wide variety of activities, including a birthday cake once a month for all birthday people that month and one or two who had birthdays during the summer when school was not in session, parties, secret pals, a monthly award called the Sammy, bowling parties, an outrageous band of "barely" musicians who would serenade staff members on their birthday wherever they could find them, and dinners at local restaurants.

Several times a year, the Home and School Club would provide lunch for the staff, usually just before major holidays. On several occasions when I sensed that the staff was stressed, I would arrange for a long lunch schedule, ask the Home and School Club for salads and desserts, and I would provide chicken breasts for barbecued chicken sandwiches. I would call on a teacher who loved to barbecue and offer to take his classes for two hours before lunch so that he could set up the barbecue and cook the chicken. It was always a hit.

I tried to start each school year with a celebration. The best was when we all met at a local yacht club for a kickoff barbecue and first day back meeting. Because it was a meeting, all the staff had to come, put down their work, and enjoy themselves. The teachers had spent the morning in their room, a number one priority, and then came for the "meeting" at the club. Here we relaxed, ate good food, and caught up with each other after the summer's adventures. The meeting consisted of introducing the new staff members and a welcome back to returning staff. We would then adjourn to the school for organizational business meetings. Five years after I left the school, teachers were still telling me how important those recreational breaks were to them.

The SAM Band   Box 2.1

Sitting in an administrative council meeting that included all administrators in the district, a usually somber affair behind closed doors, I was rocked by a cacophony of off-key music that roughly, very roughly, resembled the tune "Happy Birthday" coming from directly outside the closed door. The door swung open and in marched the SAM "band," if you could really call it a band, composed of a science teacher with a trumpet, a math teacher with a trombone, another math teacher with a drum, and a PE teacher with a tambourine. They surrounded me at the table and, drowning out the superintendent's exclamation, "What the hell!!!" proceeded to sing and play to me in celebration of my birthday. On completion and without further comment, they turned on their heels and marched "musically" out the door and shut it, leaving me to explain to my boss and colleagues that that was the SAM Band from my school. If you were on the staff they would find you on your birthday, or the day they would assign to you if your birthday was during the summer, wherever you were to give their equivalent of a rousing musical celebration.

Bowling

A line of serious bowlers sat and watched in horror as a teacher prepared to bowl a ball between her legs, blindfolded, toward 10 white pins arranged at the end of the alley. Amid howls of laughter, teams of teachers bowled lines blindfolded, with their off hand, between legs, and with their feet in a lively "competition" that required no previous experience. The event was held after school at a local bowling alley that we leased for 2 hours. Following the event, we adjourned to a local Italian restaurant for dinner and awards planned and conducted by the school SAM club. And a good time was had by all.

The Sammy

Most schools have piles of old trophies given for excellence in something sometime in the dim past. These are usually found in closets or boxes stored in the gym, and no one on the staff can remember why or who received them.

The SAM club coordinators rescued a particularly gaudy one of these abandoned icons from oblivion and brought it to a faculty meeting each month. Before the meeting staff members found slips of paper in their mailboxes requesting the nomination of a teacher for the award. On the slip the name of the nominee was written along with a description of the act that led to the nomination for this prestigious award. During the meeting a name was drawn from those nominated that month, the slip read in public, and the award presented. The other slips were similarly read and given to those not fortunate to win the drawing. During the remainder of the month, the recipient of the award was expected to keep the trophy prominently displayed in his or her room for all to see. An engraved nameplate was added and the trophy was returned at the next faculty meeting to start the process over again. Students soon realized that although this was humorous the staff took it seriously and the recipient deserved their congratulations.

The establishment and maintenance of trust is the most important task of a true leader. It is also true that without trust within the learning community widespread collegial relationships are not possible. The effective principal must constantly work to keep the level of trust high and immediately intervene when he feels that there is a threat to the hard-won trusting relationships. Successful administrators develop an intuitive understanding of trust and its importance over time. Take time to culture and nurture trust from the very beginning.

3

Learning to Change
(and Liking It)

She stood there before me, excitement written all over her face. She was literally bubbling with enthusiasm. It was contagious; I was catching the thrill, the thrill of her learning.

"You just won't believe it. I took this class at the university about cooperative learning and I was sure it wouldn't work. Look at these papers, they are the best I have ever seen. I mean, I had tried 'group work' before, thinking it was cooperative learning, and it was a mess. It was nothing like cooperative learning."

The words gushed from her all at once.

"Do you know what cooperative learning is? I mean really *know?* You should have the entire staff trained in it. You see, it's not just group work. First you . . ."

As she went on to tell me about cooperative learning, I paid close attention. I asked questions. I paraphrased. I was consumed with my own excitement of her learning. I did not let her know that I have taught hundreds of teachers about cooperative learning and written two published articles on the subject.

The principal is often referred to as the "instructional leader," and I took that seriously. Being the instructional leader does not make you an expert in anything. Remember that you cannot give what you do not have. We develop our expertise over time, but we can never be experts in everything. What we do as instructional leaders is foster learning in our staff and community. We model continuous professional growth and we evaluate our employees as they progress in their own learning. We coach teachers and students. We take care of our own learning and share the wealth.

Part of the job is to listen and revel in another person's discovery without getting in the way. If we really care, we get just as excited with their learning as we do with ours.

Change is very difficult for most people. It is especially difficult for people who think everything is going well. Many teachers, especially those who have been working at their jobs for a long time, do not see a reason for change. Partly the problem is change itself, but another major block to change is that those being asked to change do not see the reason. This is usually due to the fact that most teachers do not read in their areas of expertise.

It has been said that the phrase "teacher reader" is an oxymoron. I cannot agree more when it comes to teachers reading professional books and journals on a regular basis.

Even after 20 years as a staff developer and 14 years as an administrator, I never cease to be surprised when I ask a group of teachers, "How many of you know of the magazine *Educational Leadership?*" and I only see 5% to 10% of the hands go up. I get even less response to the same question about the magazine *Phi Delta Kappan*. If I bring up a current book, I am lucky to find one in a hundred who has even heard of the title.

If education is ever to be a true profession, we as educators must read and pay attention to the current research on how people learn and constantly update our knowledge base of our specialties. Just attending an occasional workshop will not do it. True professional growth takes place when we read, participate in training, write about what we do, and talk to colleagues about what we are learning.

The process of talking about what we are learning fits with the current research about how the brain learns. By talking to others about new information, we are processing the new knowledge and interweaving it in our permanent memory. We integrate it and validate it with what we already know.

To promote a climate for stimulating change, I used several methods to encourage reading. Some of these included encouraging journal reading, a reading club called the Reading Roundtable, and the Philosophy Club.

Encouraging Journal Reading

In my third year as a biology teacher, I read an article in *Reader's Digest* about a justice of the U.S. Supreme Court, Hugo Black. It appears that he used to read an hour a day about law. An hour a day adds up to 365 hours a year, which translates to more than nine 40-hour weeks of straight reading without a break! As a result of his reading, he became, according to many, one of the most inspired jurists in our history.

After I read about Justice Black, professional publications became important to me and I devoted one-half hour per day to this reading. In other words, I was reading about 180+ hours a year, or 4.5 40-hour weeks! I was amazed at how much I could learn in my 30-minute reading time, and my colleagues thought that I was reading continuously.

Both of us have noticed, over the years, that teachers rarely read professional literature. When I conduct staff development training throughout the United States and Canada, I always ask for a show of hands about several journals. The results show me that less than 10% of teachers even know what the *Educational Leadership* or *Phi Delta Kappan* magazines are, let alone read them. Furthermore, few teachers read professional publications in their own disciplines or even know they exist.

If I were a superintendent, I would make a policy that the district would pay for one professional journal for each teacher each year. This would not be a "perk," but rather an investment in professional development that would reach far and wide.

To promote professional reading in our schools, as principals we both constantly shared articles with our teachers. Appropriate articles were copied and distributed into the appropriate teacher's mailbox, without comment other than a note stating, "I thought you might be interested." There was no requirement for them to read them. I emphasized in staff meetings that my intent was enrichment, not remediation. I started this in my first year at New Brighton Middle School, and it was not long before I was receiving comments about the articles from most of the teachers who received them and, an added bonus, I started to receive articles from teachers.

Warning! If you encourage your staff to read, you will be held to what they read. Be ready for a different quality of professional discussion at future meetings when you begin.

Reading Roundtable

I started the Reading Roundtable as a district program in the Soquel School District in California. The idea was to get educators from the superintendent to the teachers to read educational material on a regular basis. We started with a small grant to support the purchase of books and invited people to come on a regular monthly basis. At the first meeting of the year, we chose two book titles and ordered a copy for every person who agreed to come regularly and, especially, to be there on the days we would talk about the book.

Between book days we would bring journal articles to share and discuss. Each member chose an area to become an "expert" on. During the year that person would attempt to collect as many journal articles he or she could and make copies of one or two to share with other members. As members discovered articles devoted to another member's area of expertise, they would copy and send them to the person. Thus each one of us was building an extensive collection of articles around a specific topic. When members needed new information, they would first go to the other members as a resource.

Twice a year were book discussion days, and we would provide a dinner from the grant money or potluck from the members depending on the budget. The titles we chose covered a broad range from specific educational topics to *I Can See You Naked*, a book about public speaking.

Teachers and administrators from every school in the district and the district office attended on a regular basis. At the end of the year, at the end of our last meeting, we would choose the two books for the next year.

Bill Sommers started a similar program in the Wayzata School District in Minnesota. There were several parts, beginning with a book study group for principals. At the first meeting one year, they chose the book by Peter Senge, *The Fifth Discipline* (1992), and another, with the title *Built to Last* by James Collins and Jerry Porras (1994). They decided to meet off-site and determined which chapters were going to be discussed at the next meeting. As principals, they were able to pool their experiences and talk about how to implement new ideas in their schools as they gained insight from the reading.

He also started book study groups for teachers and administrators in the high school. This provided a connection between these groups that was not about school policy and rules. The staff and administration could discuss ideas about education, leadership, and organizational structure stimulated by the reading. Since the focus was the book's ideas and their application to the school, situations rarely developed where someone became defensive.

The program was well received and went a long way to increase learning and develop a new collegiality. The administration and staff formed a true team feeling that brought a positive influence to the school.

Another program started by Bill was the exchange of book summaries, articles, and thought-provoking stories by the staff at Wayzata High School. He started by taking a poll at the school about who would like to receive summaries or articles every 3 weeks. The poll was needed to determine who was truly interested so as not to waste time and money making copies for those not interested.

Out of a staff of 84 members, the first year he had 35 people, all teachers, who signed up. The second year the group was expanded to 55 people, including several clerical, health service, and other support staff members. Staff members reported to him that people were discussing the new information in the hallways, in department meetings, and in the staff lounge. It was gratifying to hear the interchange of new ideas and information. He states that this was the start of a new learning environment on his site.

When he became principal of South High in Minneapolis in a new district, he started the same program. Out of 88 staff members, 45 teachers signed up the first year and 55 the second. He also had requests from other building principals who wished to be included, as well as the business manager for the teachers union. Again the members of the group expressed to him that great discussions were happening throughout the school.

Bill carried this idea to the parents by including research reports and educational literature in the biweekly newsletter. He also wrote extensive book summaries that he often included in a biweekly letter to the interested parents. This allowed him to educate parents about new ideas so that they could understand his philosophy and actions concerning their school.

Philosophy Club

I felt that teachers rarely took the time to talk about their profession. Teachers usually use the faculty room as a place to let off pressure, say hello, work, or just sit quietly. It is rarely used as a place to talk about educational theory, problems, or methods.

To address this need, I started the Philosophy Club, to meet on the last Wednesday of the month to provide time to meet monthly, enjoy each other, and talk about education. We would meet at a local restaurant and lounge after school. I would get there early to reserve a space and order appetizers for anyone who showed up. People would buy a beverage and we would have an informal discussion around some topic determined usually by the group. The rules were simple.

No nuts-and-bolts talk about the running of the school.

No official leader.

That's it. On several occasions I would invite a visiting educator from a local university or some other education program to come meet with us. In 7 years, I was never skunked. The largest group of teachers was 28 and the smallest was 2.

These meetings always started in a lighthearted way with some small talk and a "letting go" of the day. Soon, however, we would be deep in a discussion about something educational. Often the reason certain people showed up was to discuss a topic they were interested in. In other words, most people showed up with an agenda.

I clearly remember two specific incidents from those meetings: First was a meeting where a number of our language arts teachers were discussing a book about teaching writing in the middle school by Nancy Atwell (1988). All but one of the teachers there was enthusiastically talking about how they used the information in their classrooms and how well the process seemed to work. One teacher, one whom I would call very much a stand-and-deliver traditionalist, began to ask how the other teachers were able to implement the program. As she received the answers, she suddenly began to weep and stated that she just could not understand how it could ever work since it was so different from how she taught. The other teachers offered to coach her in the process, and after one of our longest sessions, she left in better spirits. There was always learning at those meetings.

The second incident occurred at my direction. In my first year at the middle school, I encountered an interesting situation that demonstrates what I mean by educational incest, or inbreeding of ideas.

My school was steeped in the California Writing Project. When I arrived, I was pleased to find that all the teachers were using this process with our students. It was not long, however, before I developed a serious question about how the process was interpreted by the teachers using it.

I was in a classroom watching the process in action. I was particularly interested in the fact that the teacher did not read the rough drafts with an eye for proper grammar. I asked, "When do you correct for proper grammar?" The teacher told me that only took place at the very end of the process, because to do so before would discourage the student's creativity! I was sure that she was wrong, and I had several things I could do about it. I could order a change or tell the teachers I felt it was wrong. I was not a writing teacher and felt that neither course was appropriate if I really wanted my teachers to change and feel good about it.

I chose to invite Don Rothman, the local director of the California Writing Project at the University of California at Santa Cruz, to our next Philosophy Club meeting and he agreed to come. The meeting had the largest attendance of all—28 or 32 teachers came—and it was quickly established that grammar was to be corrected at all levels, although there was no penalty for bad grammar until the final draft was completed.

To say the least, the Philosophy Club almost always resulted in deep discussion around educational topics. People used it to hone ideas and explore new directions, something that there is rarely time for in our hectic day-to-day teaching lives.

STAFF DEVELOPMENT

There is a joke that I have heard many times. It seems that two teachers died and showed up at the Pearly Gates and were met by St. Peter. He welcomed them with the statement, "Welcome to Heaven. Here you will be rewarded for eternity in a reciprocal fashion to the way your special talents were rewarded on earth. He led them to a slum, and they said, "Is this where we get to spend eternity?" "No!" he replied, "Here is where we send the millionaires who made it here." They continued on until they reached a lower-middle-class neighborhood. Again they asked the question, "Is this where we will spend eternity? "No!" he replied again. "Here is where we put the doctors and lawyers if they make it this far." They walked until they came to a beautiful area, more beautiful than they had ever experienced. There were gorgeous homes, forests, waterfalls, and all manner of treats and conveniences. Each home was full of servants. St. Peter said, "Here is what you have earned with your talents and here you will spend eternity doing what ever you wish. Welcome." The teachers looked around and said, "But we don't see any teachers. Are we the only ones?" "Oh no." he replied. "I forgot to tell you that they are not here today because once a month we send them all to hell to remind them of staff development days!"

Over the years I have discovered that teachers often become sour about staff development. I feel that this is usually due to the fact that the teachers feel that they are not in control of their own learning. Either staff development is something that is "done" to them or they do not respect the reason they are being asked to learn something new. After all, most teachers spend the entire day locked in a struggle to survive in a room full of immature human beings, and many have little control over their school lives during that time. They are in the survival mode and feel that they "know what works" as a result of the natural history of the classroom. Because their hard-won knowledge has made their difficult days survivable, the very thought of change is often received with skepticism. Learning something new often involves the sequence of finding out that they were doing something wrong for one reason or another. This is becoming more and more apparent as new strides are reported in determining how the brain learns and suggesting new ways to work with teaching and the human brain.

Learning is a humbling experience. To learn something is to admit you do not know. If trust in the experience does not exist, learning most likely will not happen. In this day and age, the public, politicians, and the media are constantly pointing out the inadequacies of public education. Teachers tend to become entrenched behind the battlements with the feeling that, after all, they are the professionals and what do outsiders really know. Time after time, educators are forced into sudden changes because of the whim of a politician. It is no wonder they do not want to change.

I can remember back when I first started teaching. I was, in my mind, an excellent teacher. I was big and strong and could control my high school class by my presence alone. I lectured and questioned and often used sarcasm as a method of reprimand, saying things like, "Can I expect an improvement or is this as good as it gets?" "Where were you standing when the brains were passed out?" Students would laugh and appear to enjoy my remarks—after all, I did not really mean them, and I was sure that they understood.

I began to study about thinking and how the brain works with Art Costa, and as part of that training I was shocked to discover that put-downs did nothing to improve students' attitudes for learning. In fact, put-downs usually set students' learning back, causing them to downshift, so to speak, in the brain, a reaction that takes time to recover from. I was very upset to discover this information, and it caused me to think back about how many students I had affected over a period of 12 years with this wrongheaded idea. I had been functioning at a level of unconscious incompetence for those years when it came to the use of sarcasm to motivate students. I was very comfortable in that state of mind because I did not know that I was doing anything wrong.

The discovery of my mistake was painful to say the least. It left me in a state of conscious incompetence. As uncomfortable as it was, at least I now knew what I had to do to correct my behavior. I had to find other ways to respond to poor student work that would encourage each person to do better without making him or her resist learning. I had to keep all of my students in that part of the brain that was the place of poets and scientists—the creative zone.

The very next day I told all of my classes about the discovery. I apologized for any pain I may have caused and told them I was going to change. I asked them to help me remember what I had to do and to point out when I fell back into old habits. I also asked them to give me feedback on how it felt for me to change. I was now functioning at a level of conscious competence and I felt awkward. This is the point where it is easy to fall back into old habits. When the room becomes confused and the teacher is struggling, he or she often retreats to the old habits that helped him or her survive in the past.

It was awkward because it was not "me" yet. I had to think about my responses, try new words, and develop new behaviors. Gradually, as I found my way, the new behavior became more familiar to me and it felt good. My students responded well and I realized that I was making progress as a teacher. Soon I no longer had to think about how I was responding; I was now at the level of unconscious competence. At least I was there as far as that one aspect of my teaching was concerned.

People often find it painful to experience self-examination, self-evaluation, and the changes suggested by the process. They fight suggestions with phrases like, "What did we used to call this?" Or, "I have been a teacher for a long time and I know what works." As educational leaders we must adroitly maneuver these people into a quest for learning, a place where nothing is held sacred and the culture of the school is one of continuous learning for all people involved. Students and adults alike are part of the learning community. Educators should expect no less from themselves than they expect from their students.

Socrates said that we should question the society we live in. He got hemlock for it. Questions cause people to react and they often become defensive. He also went on to say that the unexamined life is not worth living. If we are afraid to look closely at what we do, then the results will be like taking hemlock. Hemlock works by slowing the nervous system down until you are dead. What a metaphor that is for those of us who constantly seek the status quo!

When I was a teacher at San Lorenzo Valley High School, formal staff development was a joke. Two or three days before the designated staff development day, the principal would come to us and say something like, "Well, what do you guys want to do?"

I was a science teacher and often would like to go see some science facility such as the Lick Observatory or the nearby marine aquarium. The day would come and usually other teachers, teachers who did not care about their own development, would hear about what I was doing and ask to go along. We would head off, six teachers from disciplines such as English, foreign languages, history, PE, and science, to visit my science site. We would all have a good time, but it was not staff development.

As a principal, I was committed to doing a better job of staff development. My school had two basic staff development programs: the formal district program developed by a committee and planned out 3 years ahead and my own monthly program for my school.

Monthly Staff Development After School

When I arrived as the new principal, we had two scheduled faculty meetings a month. These were usually business meetings. I decided that one business meeting was enough if it was done correctly (see the discussion of faculty meetings in Chapter 1). The other scheduled meeting time I converted to a regular monthly staff development time. We determined the topics for these hour-long meetings at the beginning of the year. Even though an hour is not long, it did focus the importance of taking time to pursue our profession. We covered everything from assessment in the classroom to dealing with difficult people. These sessions were conducted by me, other staff members, and at times a person from outside the district. The sessions also allowed us time to follow up on districtwide staff development.

Districtwide Staff Development

The jewel in the crown of the Soquel School District was the Staff Development Committee. The first day that teachers showed up in the fall of my first year as principal of the middle school, I was approached by a teacher who quietly asked me if she could serve on the staff development committee. Remembering the situation from my old district where getting staff members to serve on their staff development committee was like pulling teeth, I readily agreed and felt myself lucky to get such a volunteer. Within an hour or so, several teachers had come to me complaining that they had heard that I had appointed a person to the committee, telling me "It is not her turn!" I began to realize that there must be something quite different about the staff development committee in this district.

The difference was that the Soquel Staff Development Committee was a well-thought-out and powerful process that led to some of the best staff development I have ever run across.

The committee consisted of three teachers from each school in the district, plus their principals, the superintendent, all assistant superintendents, the director of staff development, and a school board member. They met once a month for an entire day, during which substitutes were provided for the teachers and lunch was provided.

All staff development plans for the district were on a 3-year plan. The first year was for exploration of an area of need, followed by a year of multiple staff development around the need, and finally an implementation and evaluation year. The committee had a rotating schedule for all disciplines, so as reading moved into the second year with staff development training, science would start exploration, and math was in the final implementation and evaluation year.

The committee was broken up into four subcommittees, with one for each of the years on cycle, such as science, reading, and math. The fourth committee was called the banzai committee, named for the Japanese battle cry yelled out just before an attack—equivalent to "Charge!" in English. This committee received simple problems that could be quickly dealt with, such as choosing dates for back-to-school night or open house or developing a new process for administering mandated testing.

The fact that the committee had representatives from each school meant that each school had deep input and was kept constantly informed about every topic. Teachers in the Soquel District really supported staff development.

COACHING

It has been said that teaching is the second most private act. Teachers spend entire years with their students without ever seeing another teacher teach or having another teacher see them. There is no other profession I know that works this way. In fact, for a variety of reasons, most teachers are afraid to have others see them teach. Cognitive Coaching©, a specific peer-coaching process, was our method of choice when it came to having teachers work with other teachers for professional improvement. Cognitive Coaching© is described in detail in Chapter 6.

MANAGING CHANGE

Another consideration when making shared decisions, or any decisions for that matter, is why a change is even being considered. Most of us, after a period of time working at a particular job, develop habits of working that become part of our daily routine. These habits have evolved over the years because they seem to work and allow us to "survive" the daily grind, making our lives a little bit easier and more relaxing because we do not have to think and work as hard as we did before we developed them. When change is demanded, we know that it means more work. Change is difficult and means that we often have to throw out a program or process that is as comfortable to us as an old blanket we had as a child. So, in response to a suggestion of change, many of us fight to remain in the comfort zone.

The principal who needs to move a staff to change must keep in mind that student learning is the focus of all school decisions. Any change in the school program or in the way each teacher works must be predicated on the fact that the change is necessary to increase student learning. For that to happen, data needs to be collected about how the students are doing and a plan made to determine if the change would make any positive difference in student achievement. If the answer is yes, then the principal must sell the change to the staff, using the data and reminding them the reason that they are there is to provide each child with the best education possible.

When I arrived at my new job as principal of New Brighton Middle School, the sixth grade was semi-self-contained. Each sixth-grade student had a 4-hour core program with one teacher and then broke out of the core for PE and a series of trimester electives. The seventh-grade students had a two-period integrated language arts and social studies core with one teacher and then moved period by period to math, science, PE, and an elective. The eighth grade was like an old-fashioned high school, with students moving each period from class to class with no attempt at integration.

Research on middle school education has shown that students learn better if they can be involved with integrated subjects. This meant that instead of doing writing in language arts and history in social studies, the two could be integrated and students would write about history and so on.

I determined that I needed to integrate the eighth grade into at least one core of language arts and social studies. The eighth-grade teachers did not want to change, offering excuses like, "I'm an English teacher, not a social studies teacher. If I have to integrate, the students will not do as well since I cannot teach social studies as well as a trained social studies teacher can."

My goal was to first create eighth-grade single-teacher social studies/language arts cores and finally seventh- and eighth-grade core families in which each student would be assigned to a family composed of a core social studies/language arts teacher, a math teacher, and a science teacher, thus integrating four subjects for the students.

After much thinking, I started the change by devoting staff development time to faculty meetings sharing research on what is known about the structure of good middle schools in regards to student learning. I also distributed literature to the appropriate teachers through their mailboxes as described in Chapter 2.

The New Brighton eighth-grade core teachers made the decision to form cores to commence the following fall, and the seventh-grade teachers agreed to help them since they had been teaching as a core program for several years. The first year, several eighth-grade teachers felt that they had the expertise to teach a single-teacher two-period core, but several did not. They were the subject-specific teachers, teachers who specialized in English or social studies in their training and credentials. In those cases, we paired an English specialist with a social studies teacher who would share back-to-back programs with a common prep period for planning until they felt competent to work alone or until they retired.

The decision was made by consensus, as were most shared decisions. The process and the decision were reviewed at the end of the year, and the core program for the eighth grade was established.

Two years later, using the same technique, the seventh and eighth grades moved to the core family concept described above. The core families are still in operation today, over 6 years after I left the school, demonstrating the effectiveness of the process.

This process of establishing need, validating proposed programs, educating the staff, involving those affected by the change, providing support, and conducting ongoing evaluation produces positive long-lasting results. Those teachers involved in the above example, although concerned about the change, always supported the group's decisions enthusiastically. We never had a case of undermining or foot dragging, and in the end everyone could take credit for a job well done.

4

Classrooms Are Not
the Only Places to Learn

School should be an adventure. The idea that the classroom is the only place where all learning takes place defies logic. In fact, often classroom learning is not "real life" learning, and much of what goes on there is ignored or forgotten, for good reason. Students learn constantly, and a good school uses all the resources on and off the campus to provide a practical, real-life learning environment. Whether it is a traveling school, a field trip, or a classified employee showing kids how to fix a leaky pipe or plant a tree, it is all learning.

EXAMINING YOUR SCHOOL— WHAT IS REALLY GOING ON?

I have often wondered how presidents ever find out how the people really feel about their job. As a principal, I ran into an information block that made me think even harder about that question. When I attempted to find out what was going on in my school or tried to get an honest opinion, it seemed that I would always hear what some other person thought I wanted to hear. This makes the truth very difficult to get at. Where is the learning taking place? It is true that much learning is going on in the classroom, but there is a terrific amount going on elsewhere on the campus or in the community.

The only way I know to truly find out what is going on is to get out there and see for yourself. One of my closest friends, a principal, told me when I first became a principal, "Get out there and don't stay in your office." It was good advice. Another way to find out is to encourage teachers to tell you the creative and wonderful things that they are doing in their programs. If you encourage and reward creative work, teachers will go to the ends of the earth to demonstrate their work.

During one of my walks, I came across some students lying on the ground underneath their desks outside the classroom. They were clad in old clothes and had at their sides various colors of paint. Taped to the undersides of the desks were sheets of paper, and each child was attempting to paint a picture on the paper above his or her head. I asked what was going on and they responded by telling me that they were studying about Michelangelo and wanted to experience what it was like to paint upside down!

On other occasions I encountered similar enjoyable discoveries about my staff. There is a dark side, however, for at times you will discover things that should not be out there. I walked into a math teacher's room during instruction. The teacher was in front of the class and, unknown to her, three girls were hiding behind a bookcase reading magazines. When they saw me, one of the girls put her finger to her lips and said, "Shhhhh." The teacher was still unaware of me or the students behind the bookcase, and I knew that I had a serious problem to work on with that teacher.

UNIQUE PROGRAMS WITHIN AND WITHOUT THE DISTRICT

As a teacher, I often attempted to link students up with people in the community. At one point, I remember that I linked up a young female student with a beekeeper for a biology project. The object was to build an observation beehive for the classroom. Just when I was feeling smug about the project because she would learn about the bees, he would learn about the school, and I would get an observation hive for my classroom, the dream fell apart. Her father hit the ceiling because he did not trust the beekeeper, even though he was a married man with children, and angrily terminated the project. He even went to the principal to complain about me. This outcome, although painful at the time, did not sway me from the opinion that the education of students should not be confined to the classroom.

A more successful example is the Salmon Project at New Brighton Middle School. Charley VanderMaaten, a science teacher, wanted to involve his students in a project to help return salmon to the rivers and creeks in Santa Cruz County, California. The project requires the teacher to make trips to another school district for instruction and to purchase equipment to house the eggs and fingerlings until it is time to release them. Then the students need to be able to leave the campus with the teacher to release the young fish in nearby streams. Along with the actual raising of the fish is the painting of signs on street curbs over storm drains explaining that nothing toxic should be dumped in the drain because it flows to the creek. What a great learning experience this is for students! It is important to not forget that there is always the possibility of trouble whenever students leave the campus and are not under your direct supervision. Letting them go for good reason adds worry to the principal until they return, but it is a chance he or she should take for the sake of student learning.

As a principal, I always supported learning outside the classroom and school. When students realize that the world is the learning place, that learning is not confined to the classroom alone, they begin to adopt the habits of lifelong learners. Many schools today require students to complete a project outside the school to graduate. Some schools require a senior to adopt a national park and become an expert on it and its history or work with a senior citizens home for a semester. These projects are varied and limited only by the imagination.

An art teacher who worked at my middle school had a requirement that all art students view art outside the book and the classroom. She had lists of places in the town where students could view local artists' work. Bakeries, banks, restaurants, and other public places often hang art for public viewing, along with local museums. She was especially interested in having students' view current artwork, not just works of famous artists throughout history. This led me into an unexpected confrontation.

One day, an irate parent called me on the phone. He was fuming about the art teacher's assignment. He stated that he only wanted his daughter to view the works of the masters. He did not want her to see the "vulgar work of amateurs!" I argued that even Rembrandt was a contemporary artist at one time and asked if he would have objected to her viewing his work in a local business? There was no swaying him, and I had to tell the teacher to let this student out of the assignment without penalty. Once again it proved to me that there is no safe decision no matter what it is.

Many times, students have a skill that they can share with other students, and the pursuit of that skill takes their learning far beyond the school and community. I was starting my first year as principal of the middle school when I received a visit from a father requesting an exception to the rule that all students be enrolled in a PE program at the school. He told me that his seventh-grade son was an expert in karate and that he would like the child to leave school every day at the end of fifth period to go train with a master.

I had heard this story before in other forms. Parents attempting to pass off one thing or another as a replacement for some part of our program often exaggerated. I gave this father my standard answer, asking him to bring some kind of proof that the son was doing this sport on a regular basis. Within a day, I received calls from karate masters in England, Paris, and other parts of the world telling me that this boy was truly an up-and-coming world champion. Then the father brought me a stack of national and international karate magazines with his son's picture on the covers and feature articles defining his skills and progress.

Naturally, I let the boy adapt his school schedule to pursue his sport. I asked him if he would plan an assembly to demonstrate the sport to the school and he agreed. The assembly was wonderful and the students were surprised to discover that karate was more like dancing than fighting. We all benefited.

Another teacher approached me one spring with an idea for a class. He wanted to teach a shop class that focused on the maintenance of the school. The project was extremely successful and the school benefited with much-needed maintenance. Students did painting, electrical work, carpentry, plumbing, paving, and gardening under the direction of the district maintenance staff. We never had it so good—but remember to consult the union to make sure it is on board. The local maintenance people often will become advocates rather than adversaries if they are given the chance.

As discussed in the next section, for 3 years I taught a traveling school with another teacher. With our students, we traveled the length and breadth of California learning about life from real-life situations.

On a different occasion, another teacher and I took the students from our team-taught class titled "The Impact of Science on World History" to Canada to view the World Exposition. What a learning experience that was for all of us! For one, we did not anticipate the problems of taking 45 juveniles out of the country.

None of these programs could happen without the support of a brave and courageous principal who trusted me. There are always questions of what "could" happen on a trip, yet they supported me and I supported similar projects for my teachers when I was principal.

SCHOOLS WITHIN A SCHOOL— INTEGRATED INSTRUCTION, CORES, AND ACADEMIES

During a period when our district was going through an extremely crowded condition, with more students than rooms, a teacher friend of mine, David Weiss, and I began thinking about an alternative to teaching in the traditional classroom. He was a social studies teacher at the time and I was a science teacher. With the encouragement of a school board member, we began to think of a traveling school program. The board was looking for ways to reduce the congestion of an overcrowded campus.

Our idea was to have a set number of students that would be assigned to us all day. We would meet with those students off campus, freeing up two classrooms. We would teach them a combined history and science program while traveling to various sites around the state. The proposed class title was "California Field Studies—The History and Natural History of California." After preliminary planning, we brought the idea to a group of our colleagues for comment and they brought up many questions and concerns:

- ◆ How much will the site cost?
- ◆ What about bells?
- ◆ What about math, PE, and other required subjects?
- ◆ What about cost of travel?
- ◆ How will you get around and who pays?
- ◆ What about chaperons?
- ◆ Is it not a dumbing down of the curriculum—too much touchy-feely?

On and on they went, with us frantically taking notes and not talking.

The idea was to determine the roadblocks before we approached the powers that be for permission to teach the class. After each meeting with our ad hoc committee, we would try to address the questions that arose.

The process was the beginning of a way of working that has become a habit that served me well as a principal. I learned that after getting an idea, especially a new concept, take it to people you respect and have them look at it critically before you commit yourself. The key is to let people who think attack the idea without becoming defensive. Do not "own" it; just let people respond while you take notes. This way you will be able to address most of the questions a superintendent or school board will have before they ask them. I have also found that having a diagram to use as an illustration while talking about an idea allows a focus for people and gives you a place to take notes. Presently, I make my diagrams on a computer using the program Inspiration.

After the critique session, I return to the diagram program on the computer and adjust it using the new information, print it off, and then go out and ask for comments again.

Using this process, little by little we addressed the concerns of the committee and finally presented the full idea to the school board. The board members were ecstatic! They did not have one question or concern since we had done our homework. California Field Studies (CFS) was a reality and basically worked as follows: (CFS) was a sophomore class for students who wanted a challenge and could prove that they were responsible. We felt that it was not for students "in need" or problem students. To be selected for the program, students must fill out an application and get teachers to recommend them, just like filling out a job application. Then they would go through an interview with us. In reality, we accepted every student who could get teacher recommendation.

We limited the class to 50 students. Taking our regular class load of 30 students per period for five periods and then dividing by 12 arrived at this figure. This represents two teachers' student load per period for six periods. In reality, all teachers had one preparation period out of six and actually taught five classes. We were going to agree to take the kids all day long without the benefit of a preparation period.

We found a Christian conference center near the school that did not use its buildings during the week and leased it for a song. Dave and I wrote a curriculum integrating science, social studies, language arts, mathematics, and PE. Our idea for PE was to have students engage in physical activity as part of the program, such as bicycling, beach volleyball, and new games. We hired an aide to help us and planned integrated trips to Sacramento, Monterey, the Northern California coast, a Yosemite-Tahoe loop, and a cattle ranch. Travel was by school bus with driver volunteers, and the students earned the money for and cooked the food (this led to some interesting meals). All in all, we were way ahead of the idea of thematic and integrated teaching, since this program ran in the early 1970s.

On reflection, the lesson I learned is that there is no one "correct best" way to teach. There are many ways to teach well, and administrators must observe the results of a particular method before they criticize or praise. Keep an open mind, because the most important thing about learning is to have enthusiastic teachers with a good curriculum and enthusiastic students who cannot wait to learn. There are many ways to accomplish this. Do not think you know it all!

On another occasion, I was involved in planning and teaching an integrated thematic program for "gifted" students, a program for sophomores called "The Impact of Science on World History." This program was designed with a group of teachers, administrators, gifted students, and school board members. The two teachers, a social studies/English teacher and a science/math teacher had a two-hour back-to-back block of time. They proposed two classes that they would share with each other in a way that would allow them to integrate their subject matter around the topic. To get into the program, students had to be identified as gifted or they could *declare themselves gifted.* The class was partially funded by the Packard Foundation in California, and the success was determined by a study completed by Stanford University. Stanford discovered that not only were our students more successful in learning world history than students in traditional programs, but they also demonstrated that by the end of the program it was not possible for an outside observer to determine from the student results which students were identified gifted and which were self-nominated!

Since it has been demonstrated that students learn best when they are in integrated programs with small school units that prevent individuals from falling through the cracks, many ideas have been tested. For several years, middle schools have been integrating curriculum using the concepts of "houses," teaming, and advisories to make use of the research. High schools can be organized in the same manner.

At Wayzata High School, four teachers representing English, social studies, mathematics, and science started meeting in a study group 6 months prior to the opening of school to explore the idea of forming an interdisciplinary learning team. Their idea was for students to achieve a systemic understanding while acquiring skills in English, world history, biology, geometry, and algebra.

May 1 was the deadline for them to decide whether they wanted to take a risk and change their traditional instruction program. They decided that they wanted to change. The only administrative requirement was that the team deal with the same average number of students in a day as the rest of the school. The program was to be an alternative for students in a traditional 10th- through 12th-grade high school in which some of the students had active individual education plans (IEPs). An IEP is a legal document in California, establishing an agreement between the school district and parents about how a particular child will be taught. IEPs are dated and must be reviewed annually. An active IEP means that the student is being taught according to a current educational plan.

The team met throughout the spring and summer to develop themes around which each teacher would organize his or her program. The teachers also had the freedom to coordinate class time so that students could work together on projects. The first week of the program was dedicated to teaching creative thinking, higher-order thinking skills, and group work. Ethics, patterns, social implications, and great contributors are examples of themes chosen for the first year. To illustrate, for the ethical theme the English teacher chose specific authors who wrote about controversial issues and integrated them with the social studies teacher who provided examples in history about ethical dilemmas. Meanwhile, the math teacher demonstrated how numbers could be used to support ethical and nonethical issues and decisions, and the science teacher emphasized bioethics through genetics and environmental awareness.

The teachers taught four periods a day, in a traditional six-period day school, and used one period as common prep for coordination of curriculum and team planning. The common prep also allowed the teachers to meet with parents. The teachers were extremely positive about being able to talk to colleagues, plan together, and reflect on the day or the theme. The parents gave the administration extremely positive comments. The parents said they had never received such complete, immediate, and specific feedback on their child. Even when they disagreed on discipline or what happened to a student for not turning in work, the parents applauded the effort.

The downside was the reaction of the other staff. Even though the team members were responsible for the same number of students, many of whom the other teachers did not want in their classes, some of the other teachers could not get beyond the fact that these teachers were teaching only four periods, not five. They resented the extra prep period given the team. Another major criticism was the "not invented here" syndrome where people feel that "if I wasn't there" and "I'm not involved," it cannot be any good. As a result, the team teachers came under attack, as did the administrator in charge, contributing to a morale problem among the staff. Sometimes you have to take the flack and persevere. This uncomfortable position can be alleviated to some extent with the knowledge that you are doing what is best for each child.

As a result of the first program, some students and parents started talking about trying to implement another team to integrate the 11th grade and to continue to develop similar programs throughout the school. The teachers involved talked about how hard they were working, but they felt teaming rejuvenated their interest in professional growth and increased their respect for their colleagues involved.

Magnet schools are another way to organize schools with a large population. Research points out that high schools should have no more than 1,300 to 1,600 students. Many of us find our high schools with a population of 1,800 and higher. South High School in Minneapolis had over 1,900 students enrolled.

At South High, Bill Sommers had a number of magnet programs that drew students from the entire city as well as the school's own attendance area. The two most popular magnets were the Liberal Arts Magnet and the Open School Magnet. The Liberal Arts Magnet had many advanced placement courses and incorporated many people from the community with special interest programs. The Open School Magnet was organized around a thematic approach that included some self-paced learning where students worked on integrated projects. The Open School program was similar in philosophy to some elementary and middle schools in the district and thus was part of a natural progression for those students. The main high school program, the Comprehensive Program, was a traditional high school program that served only students from the attendance area.

Other special programs at South High included

◆ The All Nations Program, which served 125 Native American students as a school within a school. This program taught Ojibway language, drum and dance, and American history from a Native American perspective and had a support system built in where students could discuss personal problems with adults who they knew and trusted.

◆ The Mothers, Infants, and Child Education (MICE) program, designed specifically for teenage mothers with children, which served about 20 students per year.

◆ The Mall of America program: In the spirit of involving students in real-life situations, some students attended school at the Mall of America. Five school districts cooperated to fund this school. It not only offered the traditional English, social studies, science, and math classes but also had classes that connected to businesses.

The goal was to provide niches for students. We want to find a place for each student to feel connected to our school. The efforts of individual teachers and their passion for teaching children were the main reasons these programs worked. None of them was established by an administrative edict.

Urban high schools face a serious problem with dropouts, and South High School is no exception. When Bill Sommers first came to South High, he discovered that the school had over 250 dropouts during one school year. There were many factors that we could use for excuses, but the only obvious option was to meet the problem head on and do something about it. James Comer of Yale University said, "No significant learning happens without a significant relationship" (quoted in Payne, 1995, p. 61). Five staff members stepped forward and used this theme to address the dropout problem. Bill said, "I don't care what you teach as long as you build a relationship with your students. I want them to know someone misses them if they leave." He thought that it does not matter what you teach if the students do not come to school.

The original team consisted of teachers from English, social studies, physical science, and PE/health. Two teachers taught the majority of the students in math. Ninth-grade students who lived in the attendance area were candidates for this program. One third of the students involved had not passed either reading or math on state-mandated tests, one third of the students had passed only one of the state tests, and one third of students had passed both tests.

The program started as a result of 85 students and 15 adults creating a program to retain students. Bob Chadwick and Bill Sommers facilitated this group for one day in the spring of the new year. Bill, as principal, opened the meeting stating that if he knew how to retain more students he would have already done so. He told the students that they were the experts and asked for their help in creating a program that would retain more students in school.

The first year got off to a difficult start. Two administrators who had worked closely with the team were unavailable from the start. One of them had died the second week of school and the other was out because of a car accident 3 weeks into the school year. By the third trimester, however, the team had responded to most of the problems. By the end of the year the program had cut the dropout rate in half. The central office demographers commented that they could not assign as many students the next year because the school had not lost as many as normal. That was good news.

The process involved forming long-lasting relationships with each student in the Comprehensive Program. The "families" created by this process provided time for problem solving and behavior modification for each student.

In 1998, the following year, the team increased the retention rate for students and had several students from the first team come back for study days. In the third year, there was to be another team formed for ninth-grade students and the longer-term prospects include expanding the team to the 10th grade, possibly with a modified Waldorf approach.

ATTENDING TO MULTIPLE INTELLIGENCES

Recently, an assistant superintendent told me that I should no longer attend to the idea of multiple intelligences because it is passé. This statement demonstrates to me one of the major problems in our country's educational policy—in America we tend to jump "whole hog" from one educational "fad" to another. I once heard a statement attributed to Edwin DeBono, the thinking guru from England, that went something like this: "I hope that the American educational system never gets caught up in the thinking skills concept because, if they do, like everything else they do, it will become a fad and fads die out sooner or later." That is so true from my own experience. I think that it is due to the fact that in American education, we are always looking for "the answer," a magic bullet that will cure all of our educational wrongs with one simple shot. The problem is encompassed by the phrase I heard from my friend Doug Slonkowski: "For every complex problem there is a simple answer, and it is wrong!"

The concept of multiple intelligences (MI) is one of those "fads" that the educational system bought and fell head over heels in love with. It was thought to be "the magic bullet" of the 1990s. When this happened, many consultants and pioneering teachers jumped on the bandwagon and began to be the MI gurus. Many of these trainers developed their own flawed interpretations of a complex process and taught them to teachers. As an example, the process of teaching reading using the "whole language" approach was undermined by bad training giving a good process a negative reputation and sending educators looking for another "best" way to teach reading without fully understanding why a good program was not working. Education is full of "experts." I once heard Richard Daggett say that if you have a good idea about how to work with students do not name it, because if you do, someone will do it wrong and thus give the good idea a bad name, and sooner or later it will fall out of grace because of that.

In my teaching and administrative experience, I know that each student learns differently from others and that each student has his or her own special talents. This knowledge leads me to believe that attending to the concept of multiple intelligences can help all students learn more efficiently as well as helping each student to remain interested in what he or she is encountering during the school day. Because I know that research says all people learn differently, my instincts tell me that every program should have a component that attends to multiple intelligences. This also means that each teacher and administrator has the responsibility to keep up-to-date with current research and proof about how many approaches to teaching and learning work. I would also encourage schools to engage in action research projects to help confirm how programs and ideas are working.

If something works well, it should not be tossed out unless you have something that works better to replace it.

HOME SCHOOLING

One of the more difficult concepts that principals deal with today that was not a problem a generation ago is that of home schooling. Today it is a growing trend. I think the current popularity of home schooling is due to public perceptions, for whatever reason, that public schools are failing or public schools are not teaching the values of some families or religions. Regardless of the reason, the concept seems to be frowned on by the administration and faculty of the public school system.

Much of the disdain comes from the demands that many home schoolers bring to the district. In the Soquel School District a home-schooled student could demand to take certain classes at the school, go on field trips with classes that he or she was not part of, participate in sports, and attend extracurricular activities such as dances and clubs. The problems with the home school/public school relationship stem from the fact that the home-schooled student is not enrolled in the school. As a result the school does not get paid for the student and there is the potential for a discipline problem with the student who attends school programs without being officially part of the school. The potential exists because there is no real connection to the school. If home-schooled children disobey during an activity, they can thumb their noses at the person in charge because they do not have to go back to the school and receive further consequences for their behavior.

Schools should attend to these students as best they can and help the home-schooling parents work with their children. This amounts to an outreach program where the school can take the lead and demonstrate why and how public education should be considered a professional and competent organization.

The school can provide workshops for parents on methods of teaching, provide books, help parents with curriculum, and involve home-schooled children in a positive interaction with the rest of the students. I have discovered that many of these students sooner or later return to the public campus when the burden of teaching at home becomes too much. Remember, there are many famous people who were educated at home. No one person knows what is best for each child.

ART IN THE COMMUNITY

As mentioned before, many businesses display art from local community members. Artworks are found in banks, restaurants, coffeehouses, and other businesses. Much of the art on display is worthy of note and teachers can make good use of it by providing opportunities for their students to get credit for viewing local art. Encourage local businesses to notify the school when new displays are put up and then have the art teacher view the work to determine the appropriateness of the material for students. Students can be given a map of the area with art locations marked. They can view the art on their way to or from school and write an observation report for credit.

CAREER DAY

It is within our responsibility to provide students with career education. Most schools have some form of career day for their students. It affords the school with a good opportunity to make partnerships with the community. It is relatively easy to get volunteers from the parents of the students in the school to present a one-hour overview of their profession or craft. Do not ignore the art community. There are usually artists making a full-time or part-time living with their skills. In every case, be sure to schedule a credentialed teacher to be in the room with the community member. It is not legal for a noncredentialed person to be alone with students.

MINI-COURSES INVOLVING
COMMUNITY MEMBERS AS TEACHERS

One of the most popular programs at my middle school was conceived and organized by my vice principal, Stan Bovee. The mini-course program was designed to provide an alternative learning experience to students that differed from the regular curriculum. We chose to do it at two times in the year, spring and fall, when regular school began to drag and students were becoming tired of the routine.

Mini-courses allowed students to learn ideas and skills from the real world taught by members of the local community. Although this seems similar to career day, mini-courses had more depth. Whereas career day provided students with a one-hour overview, mini-courses ran two half days, usually spaced a week apart, and involved every student and many teachers and community members.

The teachers and community were surveyed for ideas for the program. Each program would run for a couple of hours on two days and be taught by a credentialed teacher or by a community member with a credentialed teacher sitting in the room. Some of the programs included photography, horse vaulting, veterinary science, police science, law, medicine, art, various sports activities, and music. Each student had to pick two programs to attend.

A week before the sessions began, each community member participating had to come to the school and for training in what was and was not acceptable as well as how to work with children. The benefits went far beyond just providing students with an alternative. Usually the community "teachers" were astounded to find out how difficult it was to work with a classroom full of middle school children. They always left the program with a huge respect for the teachers and public schools.

One caution: be sure to monitor what and how each program is taught. We allowed a women's self-defense program one year, and the teacher used very descriptive and graphic language that was not appropriate. We also had to provide backup programs in case some volunteer did not show up or was ill.

5

Tsunami—Riding the Wave of Change Without Drowning

It is one of those days in January, calm, beautiful, kids all in class, bells all working—it does not get any better. Your secretary buzzes you to tell you that the business manager is on Line 1. A chill runs down your back as you reach for the phone and punch the blinking light that represents Line 1.

"Hey Dick, how's it going?" you say merrily.

"Not so good for you or me, Dave. We've got problems."

He goes on to explain that he just heard from the state budget office. The state did not get the income expected and so we all have to cut 12% from our budgets. Immediately! He wants a budget plan within 48 hours! The message brings you to attention, your heart racing and your mind spinning.

Here is the situation. By January you have actually committed most of your budget by buying books and supplies for the year. Teachers have been contracted for and aides have been hired. You could panic but you do not because you know how to handle the tsunami.

The first thing you do is call together your personal advisory team, in my case the vice principal, the counselor, and my secretary, to tell them what has happened. My secretary brings in the budget sheets and we begin to brainstorm. I keep notes on the large chart pack that hangs on the back of my door so that it is available when the door is closed.

We total up all available uncommitted funds from all accounts. We then look at future plans and programs. Items like new equipment purchases will have to wait. Only emergency maintenance will continue. The copy machine is shut down for the moment. All classroom budgets are frozen. The office budget is frozen. In short we look at everything and come up with approximately 15% that we can draw on.

The next step is to go to the staff. I call an emergency staff meeting and tell them *everything*. Then I open the meeting up to the staff. I tell them here is the pot of money, all of it. I explain to them the bare minimum that I need to run the office for the remainder of the year. The staff helps prioritize what they feel they must have and we determine an order of purchases according to need, with the most necessary items on top. The idea is that we will spend money only when we have the expenses in the prioritized order.

Finally, we go to the Home and School Club and site council leaders to inform them of the emergency. They agree to look closely at their money to see what they can do to help and agree to support the prioritized list as funds become available.

The following day, I take the plan to the district office. The business manager tells me that it looks good and that he will let me know if more funds become available.

I made the deadline. We are not happy, but we are satisfied that everyone was involved and shared in the sacrifices that were needed to meet the challenge. We survived another tsunami by being prepared to deal with sudden change.

ESSENTIAL QUESTIONS FOR CHANGE
—FIRST, WHY? SECOND, WHAT?

In Chapter 3, we began talking about the change process. Change is not only difficult but the reasons for change have to be clear and well thought out. Most people resist change as long as the situation that they find themselves in is tolerable, even if it is only barely tolerable. Change is work so it is important to bring as many of your staff as you can along with you when change is needed. If only a few people participate in the change, they will soon feel the stress of the extra work. The original excitement of those involved will wear off and the workers will begin to look at the nonworkers and wonder if the change is worth it. All involved parties need to understand why change is necessary. They need to understand why the change will make things better for students in the long run over what is already in place.

It is my experience that change does not start with a small group of enthusiastic change leaders and then spread to the rest of the school or district. This process, often called *strategic planning*, is based on the idea that a small group is easier to work with than a large one. The problem is that when a small group makes decisions for a large group, the members of the larger group miss out on the discussions about the need to change and thus have to take the word of the smaller group for the needs and the plan, even if they were consulted during the process. The result is no different from top down. When this model is used, usually the small group burns out after several years and the other members of the educational community stay right where they were as comfortable spectators because they were left out of the loop. They are not clear about the project needs because they were not personally involved.

When I arrived at New Brighton Middle School (NBMS), I was confronted by a team of teachers who told me that the school used to be bad and now was good. I was told that NBMS was considered by most to be the best in the county and that I should not change it in any way. They even quoted the old adage, "If it ain't broke don't fix it!" Yet the school was dwelling in the past in many areas, especially special education, reading, math curriculum, and writing methodology.

As mentioned earlier, I felt that we needed to change our homeroom program, which was too short—10 minutes—and attached to first period, so that many teachers simply ignored homeroom time and used the extra 10 minutes for teaching. I also felt that we needed to convert the eighth-grade language arts and social studies programs to an integrated core program.

My challenge was how to convince the entire staff, or at least 95% of them, that change was needed. I used several methods, including a graphic tool that I had learned from a colleague. I prepared by spending time thinking about all my experiences with change as an educator. I researched my own journals and used journal writing to enhance my thinking. In short, I wanted to plan thoroughly before I started.

You Don't Have to Convince Everyone to Be Successful   Box 5.1

No matter how hard you work at bringing "everyone" along, there will be some (it is to be hoped only one or two) who will resist to the very end. I have found that if I can get at least 80% of those involved agreeing and working together toward change, I have succeeded.

I searched professional journals such as *Educational Leadership* and *Phi Delta Kappan* for articles about current thinking in my perceived areas of change. I copied these articles and just put them in teachers' mailboxes without comment beyond a note that simply said, "I thought you might find this interesting." This did several things, as described previously:

1. I demonstrated to the staff that I read and value current research. I have observed over my 20+ years in the classroom that teachers rarely read research about their fields. My action demonstrated to the staff that I valued them and thought that they were professionals who would read and think about the articles.

2. I followed up with departmental discussions about the articles or at the very least asked for feedback from the teachers who received articles. This process began to expand my staff's knowledge about their own disciplines and current best practice in education and illustrated my philosophy about education in general and NBMS in particular.

I knew that I was making headway when I began to receive articles from the staff. What a joy! I also began to discuss various topics at the Philosophy Club meetings (see the section of the Philosophy Club in Chapter 3) and had good conversations demonstrating the teacher's expanded thinking.

After several months, I decided to attack the idea of change directly on a staff development day. The tool I used was a three-chart method using standard chart paper. I prepared three charts ahead of time. The charts were placed one on top of the other on the chart stand. The first chart was labeled "5 Years Ago" and was what the teachers saw as they entered the room (Figure 5.1).

Figure 5.1.

I started by asking the teachers to divide into table groups with at least one teacher with 5 years' experience or more at each table. I also asked that at least one of the veteran teachers at each table be one who had been at NBMS for 5 years or longer. I asked those in each table group to hold a 5- to 10-minute discussion about what they remembered education in California and especially at NBMS was like 5 years before. When I perceived that the discussions were winding down, I began to collect their responses on the chart labeled "5 Years Ago" with the statements written in alternating dark colors. This chart was then placed on the wall for all to see, revealing Chart 2 (Figure 5.2).

I told the table groups that next I wanted them to discuss what was different about education in California and NBMS today from 5

Figure 5.2.

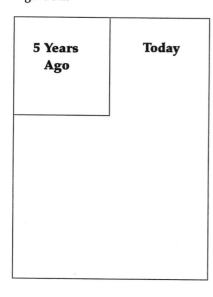

years before. After their discussion I again collected their responses and then placed the chart on the wall next to the first chart. I stressed that what they have demonstrated was that there was a difference, a change, from what we were doing 5 years ago and today. I also pointed out that the small box on Chart 2 represented what we did 5 years ago and that what we were doing today we were doing because of what we had learned 5 years ago. The present was built on the past. I also pointed out that the change was always made in hopes of doing what we do better, that we were constantly trying to improve education for our students.

When the second chart was removed from the stand and placed on the wall, it revealed the final chart (Figure 5.3). This chart was labeled "5 Years From Today" and had two boxes in the upper left. I asked them to consider that if what we do today was based on what we did and learned 5 years ago, or even yesterday for that matter, what would they expect education to look like in 5 years? I pointed to the boxes in the upper left and reminded them that they were metaphors representing the past and the present.

Again, I collected their responses. It was gratifying that in every case the groups projected changes to what we were doing. The staff saw that constructive change is not capricious but reasonable if done for the right reasons and based on experience and sound evaluation.

As a consultant, whenever I have conducted this exercise I have found that there is much conjecture about the future and almost everyone in the room agrees that change is a certainty. Participants find that it is difficult to deny that if the world is changing then their own school or district must change to keep up and that change must be built around a systematic process of determining what change is necessary.

Figure 5.3.

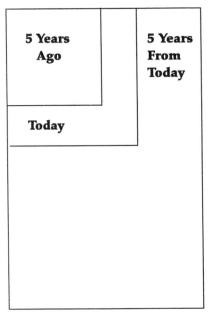

The final step in the process is to look at the current state of the school and district and determine areas that may need to change. At this point, I rearrange the table groups into homogeneous teams by discipline. I ask them to examine their programs for areas of strength and weakness and then to determine what priority they may assign to items on their list for examining possible changes to pursue.

Finally, I have them form heterogeneous groups to share change possibilities across disciplines and add another step, which I learned from Bob Chadwick, of asking them to consider three questions in order.

1. What is the worst possible outcome if we never changed what we are doing?
2. What is the worst possible outcome if we do change what we are doing?
3. What is the best possible outcome if we change what we are doing?

These statements are written on chart paper and saved to use in other planning meetings.

Once change and a priority have been agreed on, the staff must decide how to pursue the changes. I must point out that after this process is over the staff may decide that no change is necessary in some areas after all. If you do not agree, this is not the time to state your opinion. Instead, you pull back and begin the education process again.

GETTING STARTED WITH CHANGE

A good way to begin is for you and the staff to collect all you can about the changes being considered. In every case, note that you must have an assessed series of facts about what you have done or are considering doing. This means that you and the staff may have to learn how to do effective assessment.

As an example, if you are considering a change to the class schedule a number of questions must be answered:

1. How is our program working now and how are our students doing? How do we know this?
2. What do other schools do with their schedules and how well do they work? How do they know?
3. What research is out there that could help us with our decision? How do we know that the research is valid?
4. How would each schedule we look at affect our school's present program?

Figure 5.4. New Gameboard of Change

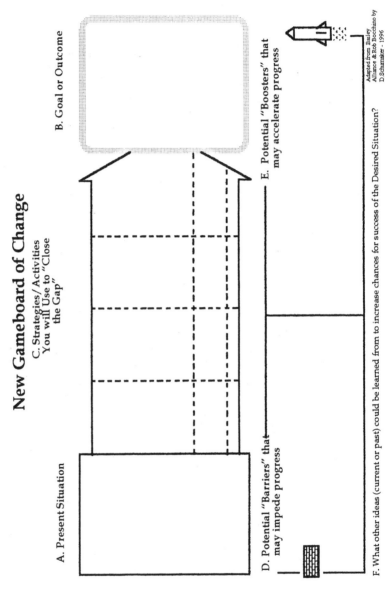

New Gameboard of Change

B. Goal or Outcome

C. Strategies/Activities
You will Use to "Close
the Gap"

A. Present Situation

E. Potential "Boosters" that
may accelerate progress

D. Potential "Barriers" that
may impede progress

F. What other ideas (current or past) could be learned from to increase chances for success of the Desired Situation?

Adapted from Bailey
Alliance & Rob Bocchino by
D.Schumaker - 1996

SOURCE: Created by Suzanne Bailey for workshop use. Reprinted with permission.

5. If we implement a new program, how will we know if it is working?

There is another tool that I use with a staff that I bring in at this time. Called "The Game Board of Change," it comes from Suzanne Bailey of the Bailey Alliance (Figure 5.4).

CHANGE MODELS, MENTAL MAPS

For working with individuals in a change situation, I have discovered another tool that works very well. The process is based on the formation of a mental map that involves both kinesthetic and visualization techniques; I learned it also from Suzanne Bailey. The following is an example of how it works:

A teacher came to me one day stating that she was not happy with her career. She stated that she wanted to do something else with her life. I asked her if she knew what she wanted to do, and she said that she wanted to teach art instead of history. I wanted to know what was holding her back. She said that it was the fact that she did not have the proper credential.

At this point, I could see that she was stuck in a situation and did not know which way to turn, so I asked her if she would take a walk with me. She agreed and we went outside to a place that was somewhat private. I then asked her to stand at a spot that I indicated on the ground.

We stood there together and I asked her to think about the situation she was trapped in at the moment. Next I asked her to look at an imaginary line on the ground extending away from where she was standing off into the distance. I told her that this line represented time and that I wanted her to walk along that time line with me until she came to a place in the future where she could imagine herself in a room teaching art.

We walked for about 20 feet and she paused. She stated to me that this was the point at which she just received her credential in art. I asked how long that was and she responded that it was about 2 years.

I asked her to turn and look back toward the point where we started that represented today and think about how that felt considering the situation she had been in. We discussed that point and she mentioned that at least now she had the option to do what she wanted to do and that her next step would be to seek a position as an art teacher.

We continued to walk into the "future" for a couple of steps and she stopped and told me, "I have my art job and I am in my classroom and it feels great."

At this point, I had her look back again and feel the good feeling while she composed a message that she could send back from the future. The message would state her feelings about the change and include one or two steps that she could take to start down the path toward the future she envisioned.

This last step is crucial. Dreaming is not productive in itself without something tangible to help us along the path to realize our dreams. You most likely know someone who is nothing but a dreamer, and he or she sits day after day in a stagnant situation wishing for a new life. Such people often use a statement like, "I just have to get my act together." They rarely do.

Some people would not respond well to the previous example, thinking it too "touchy-feely." I have found out by experience that almost everyone thinks more clearly while walking around and talking. So if you have a person stuck in a place and in need of change, ask him or her to take a walk with you as you talk about it.

TRANSITION—HONORING THE FEELING OF LOSS WITHOUT LOSING ALL YOUR TEDDY BEARS

Once the change is on the way, you must keep in mind that no matter how well prepared a staff is there will be many who will be uncomfortable with the change. Keep in mind the problems of discovering incompetence and changing to competence as described to me by Art Costa (see the example in Chapter 3):

◆ When you are doing something and it is not right and you do not know that it is not right, you are functioning at a level of *unconscious incompetence* and you are very comfortable.

◆ When you discover that what you had been doing is wrong, for whatever reason, you are suddenly aware that you are functioning at a level of conscious *incompetence* and you are very uncomfortable.

◆ When you learn a new way of doing what you had been doing wrong and it seems right, you are now functioning at a level of *conscious competence* and it feels awkward and you are still uncomfortable.

◆ Finally, when you have internalized that new concept and are functioning automatically in that regard, you are functioning at a level of *unconscious incompetence* and you are very comfortable again.

The point of greatest concern in this metaphor is at the third stage, conscious competence. Here the individual feels awkward and has to think of every move. I drive a horse and carriage. When I first started to drive, I held the reins in both hands. It became very easy for me to do what I wanted to do with the horse while holding the reins this way—it was a habit of mind and body. The problem was that if I wanted to improve and be more effective in more difficult situations as well as at higher speeds over longer distances, I had to learn a new way of holding the reins. The new way seemed so difficult, whereas using the old way I did not have to think, I just did it. I had to think of everything at once while learning a new method of holding the reins. I had to think about what each hand was doing at any one moment as well as how the horse was responding. I often fell back into the old method.

My instructor, Linda Fairbanks, provided gentle reminders about my rein handling. She kept nudging me back to the new hold whenever she saw me slip back, until finally, one day, I realized that when I picked up my reins I automatically held them in the new way without thinking. In fact, it felt very comfortable and easy for me to use. I was beginning to reach the level of unconscious competence.

Expect that as your staff begins to implement change they will feel the discomfort and, as depicted in the children's book *Ira Sleeps Over* by Bernard Waber (1972), will need to hold on to some teddy bears. I am sure that you all had some favorite toy that you kept with you far beyond childhood because it just felt good, even though you knew that it was childish. Eventually, you put it away as you learned new things and became more secure. When making a change, we cannot ask a staff to drop everything from the past practice at once. The staff must understand that the change will happen totally but not suddenly. A few teddy bears will be allowed for a time while the main practice becomes a habit of mind and then, eventually, the teddy bears can be put away.

William Bridges, in his book *Managing Transitions, Making the Most of Change* (1991), states,

> When endings take place, people get angry, sad, frightened, depressed, confused. These emotional states can be mistaken for bad morale, but they aren't. They are the *signs of grieving,* the natural sequence of emotions people go through when they lose someone or something they love. The same feeling happens when they lose something that works well for them. (p. 129)

The grief is no different from when you lose a favorite pet or object, and if the change is too traumatic people can feel as if they lost a loved one. I remember a time while I was working for the federal Youth Conservation Program and attending a training in Monterey, California. One person, an American Indian, had spent her entire life at the bottom of the Grand Canyon. She was about 30 years old and a mature adult. To attend the training, she was helicoptered to the airport from the bottom of the canyon and flown over the mountains to the edge of the ocean, which she had never seen before. She was then transported by car through the largest city she had ever seen to a conference attended by many more people than she had ever seen in one place at one time. She was so overcome by the shock of it all that she could not eat or sleep. She was struggling to function. She was displaying all of the symptoms of grieving displayed by a person who lost a relative.

People struggling with symptoms of grief are found in many situations—in families that have lost a member, in organizations where a popular leader has left, in school districts where a new superintendent is making big changes. When you take over a position as principal from a popular predecessor, you may encounter grieving in the form of mistrust and anger. Grief also results when you do away with something perceived as popular by the staff.

The change brought on when you are placed in the position of assigning a popular staff person to an assistance plan for his or her failure to meet the standards of the district as a teacher is an example. This person has been determined to be a poor teacher and you may have to let him or her go. The problem occurs when the staff finds out and only hears the teacher's side of the story. You have your hands tied and must keep quiet because it is a confidential personnel issue. Some staff members may become angry even if they know, deep down, that you are right. If the popular teacher is fired or quits, these staff members may also cause problems for the newly hired replacement.

The only way I know to deal with this is based on the goodwill bank described in Chapter 2. If you have done your job and been fair and open with the staff, they will usually realize that you must have a good reason for your decision.

In summary, the change process takes time. Start with research, examination of the future state in relation to the present state, and then set goals. The people who are affected need to know why change is needed and they need support and training. They often resist leaving their comfortable old ways for the new and often go through a grieving process as if they had lost a loved one. If they are allowed to take a "few old things" along for the trip, however, the grieving process can be relieved somewhat. They must keep in mind that in the long run the "few old things" may have to be discarded at some point if they prove to be unworkable, but by that time they will be so comfortable with the results of the changes made it will not matter to them. In all ways, seek and maintain trust.

TRAILBLAZERS, PIONEERS, SETTLERS, STAY-AT-HOMES, AND SABOTEURS

Saboteurs are another source of problems to the principal. Phil Schlechty spoke at a workshop I attended about change and the basic behaviors exhibited by teachers when they are confronted with a different way of doing something. The list is composed of trailblazers, pioneers, settlers, stay-at-homes, and saboteurs.

Trailblazers make up a small group of teachers or administrators who will try almost anything. They are the ones who go off to a conference or workshop and return ready to totally change their program or the whole school at a moment's notice, as long as it sounds like an improvement. I was often a trailblazer. I would come back to the science department from a conference and bug everyone about how we should do things differently. My colleagues would roll their eyes and whisper to each other, "There goes Schumaker again."

Trailblazers are usually not respected by the other members when it comes to recommending direction for the organization. They are usually ready to change direction on a dime if they are given a good reason and see a way to go.

Pioneers follow trailblazers only after they see that there is a possibility of success, as demonstrated by the trailblazer. Pioneers often move on after a time, but they are more stable than trailblazers. This is the other category that I fit into easily. After watching a colleague develop a good marine science program at a nearby high school, I followed, developing my program around the way he was doing his. It was very successful and exciting for my school and me.

Settlers are people who do not change easily and will do so only after it seems safe to make the move. I have never been a settler, but I think that they make up the bulk of any staff. I remember an English teacher who was nudged into a language arts/social studies core program. The purpose of the program was to integrate the two subjects and this teacher refused to do the integration. Each day she would teach English during the first hour of the block and social studies during the second. In my discussions with her about her resistance to the change, she would tell me that she could see no real reason for change. She believed that students learned better when they were not "confused" about whether the lesson was English or social studies. Only after the other core students continued to score higher on standardized tests than hers did she change. After the change, she became a firm settler in the new process. When working with settlers, remember they do not change often but change is possible with lots of proof and effective examples.

Those who refuse change altogether, and there are some of these on every staff, are refereed to by Schlechty as "stay-at-homes." You may as well forget about getting these people to move willingly and without much complaint. Most will feel that they are doing just fine and doing a good job, so why change? When I began my teaching career, I worked with a stay-at-home. She taught biology the same way every day of every year. Her lesson plan book was well worn and obviously used every year for a number of years. It was not organized by date but by week: Week 1, Week 2 . . . Every week was taught the same way. Monday: read the chapter quietly; Tuesday: read the chapter out loud; Wednesday: do the questions at the end of the chapter; Thursday: do a lab experiment; Friday: take a test. No matter what, she would not change, not even with pressure from the principal. Most of the students in her classes loved her and she considered herself very successful as a teacher. She could see no reason to change.

Finally, there are the saboteurs. These are often former trailblazers. They became disenfranchised for some reason within the school or district or just burned out in general and are angry. Many times they feel that they tried to change a bad system and finally realized the effort was useless. They do not trust the leaders and feel that they know better. Even though they know better, they will do nothing to help. They work to destroy change. They are dangerous in that they appear supportive to your face but work against you and change behind your back. They do their work in the parking lot or lunchroom, never at an open meeting. They also are among the first to get the attention of new teachers, attempting to sway them away from you and your goals.

I remember one saboteur specifically. She would often drop into my office to tell me how well I was doing and how much she supported me, yet at faculty meetings she would always vote with the majority. If she could, she would vote against something I was attempting to do, but never in the minority. After such a vote, she would inevitably drop by and tell me that she really supported my point but had to vote the way she did because she had to "live with her colleagues."

After one meeting where we all agreed to a certain procedure, I discovered that she went out and began to immediately undermine our decision. As soon as I could, I cornered her privately and confronted her with what I had heard. I did not give her time to explain. I reminded her of the rule about undermining and pointed out that she had ample time to give her input during meetings with the staff and that my door was always open. I let her know how much I disliked her tactics, that I expected her to stop, and that if I was wrong she should make an appointment with me to talk about it. I then walked away. This was not a time for discussion, and it was not the time for weasel words. Do not couch such discussions in statements like, "I know you have good ideas." Or, "I hope that what I have heard isn't true because I respect you but . . ." Instead, you should say what you mean and make it brief and to the point.

I despise these people for their sneakiness. The only way I have found to deal with them is to confront them at every turn and immediately on finding out about an undermining act. Remember the rule, "You do not have the right to undermine." In other words, you can make it uncomfortable for them if you let them know that you will call them on their deceptions.

LOSING AND REPLACING KEY STAFF MEMBERS

It was 3 days before the opening of school. The teachers had been back to New Brighton Middle School officially for 2 days, and I was feeling cool, calm, and happy. Everything was in place for another year. New teachers were hired, the schedule was complete, and students were dropping by to look at the posted class lists to see who their teachers would be. Leaning back in my chair feeling smug, I was reflecting on how well the beginning was going when in she walked.

I smiled and said hello to my math department head, one of the best math teachers on the staff—popular and effective. "How are you this fine day?" I asked.

She replied, "I'm turning in my resignation because I just took another job. I am moving to a new city. I just wanted to let you know."

I was stunned. I sat there a moment absorbing what she said. "You're kidding!" I responded.

"No, I just was waiting to be sure that the school board in my new district approved my contract. I didn't want to quit until I was sure of a new job."

I cannot tell you how angry I became. I was flattened by the decision because of her thoughtlessness for the students she was responsible for.

The situation she left me in was as follows:

◆ It was almost September and school opened officially in 2 days.

◆ Schools in the area had already hired new teachers for the year and the available pool of prospects was very small.

◆ Good math teachers were very difficult to find at best, let alone at the last minute.

◆ The official hiring policy for the district meant that it would take me a minimum of 4 weeks to complete the process.

◆ Long-term substitutes were limited in the amount of time that they could work before they had to be considered regular members of the staff.

◆ There were very few qualified substitutes on the list that I could rely on.

◆ What was I going to do to control myself so that I would not kill her or collapse with a stroke?

As she walked away without a care in the world, I began to plan. There was no use waiting. The tsunami had hit and change was afoot!

First, I called together my advisory group: the vice principal, the counselor, and my secretary. They came to my office immediately and we attacked the problem. I called the superintendent and asked for a meeting with her because I needed to shortcut the hiring process. She agreed and soon we had a plan for a fast hire. After going through several substitutes, we were able to hire a good math teacher. In the long run, the students did suffer, however. The students in the classes affected trailed their fellow students from other teachers' classes academically throughout the year.

As I said, I cannot tell you how angry this situation made me. Teachers expect that we will honor our commitments to them, adhere to their contracts, and keep our word. They demand to be told that they are rehired by mid-March in our state (California), yet some seem to forget that they are under contract. The math teacher who quit just days before the students arrived on campus could not understand my anger. She did not think of her students.

The truth of the matter is that no matter how good you are to your very best staff members, some key person seems to leave every year. Usually they are polite and think that they are giving you plenty of warning about an impending departure by informing you in late May or June. Even this consideration is too late, again because of the hiring processes imposed by districts and the availability of good teachers.

If you want to be able to get the best teacher for your students, you must be looking by mid-March or earlier. The reason is obvious: Most teachers are looking for jobs at that time because that is the time most schools are looking for teachers. New teachers are anticipating credentials and diplomas in June and want to get a jump on the job market.

To overcome these problems, I do two things:

◆ Educate the teachers during a faculty meeting in February about the hiring process and emphasize the students' need for good teachers. Let them know that you need as much lead time as possible if you are to get a good replacement for them.

◆ Talk to the superintendent about the necessity of getting the best teachers for your students by allowing maximum credit for experience on the salary scale and streamlining the hiring process. My superintendent helped guide the school board to the decision that the cheapest (usually the youngest and least experienced) teacher is not who we wanted. If we were to get the best, we had to hire the good, experienced teacher, and to entice him or her to work for us we had to give as much credit on the salary schedule as we felt we could afford. In California, we have to grant up to 5 years' experience. My district allowed me to make the decision of how much credit to give. For a good bilingual or math teacher, I have granted up to 8 years' credit.

The point is that you are in the business of seeing that your students get the very best education they can. To do that you need the best teachers for them at every turn. To do that you must educate your staff and district in ways to maintain a competent, effective teacher force.

DEALING WITH THE DEATH OF A STUDENT

Nothing is more traumatic to the school community than the death of a student or current school employee. Although the death of an adult is bad enough, the death of a child deeply disturbs the school culture, as it should. It seems so wrong that a young life should be so prematurely ended.

I was patrolling the campus early one morning when I received word that one of our students had been hit by a truck near the campus. The student had been on his way to school on a city bus, and when he exited the bus he stepped out from the front of the vehicle into the oncoming traffic, where he was struck by a pickup truck passing the bus.

Nothing in all my experience had prepared me for this, but I began to act on instinct. I radioed my vice principal and found that he was already on the site of the accident. I asked if he needed help. He responded that he was OK and that the emergency vehicles were already there. He told me who the student was and that he was very badly injured—unconscious—and that it was a very grave situation.

We decided to pull back slightly and keep students from rushing to the site.

Communication System   Box 5.2

I cannot overemphasize the importance of having a good two-way communication system in any school today. We used a two-way radio system with the base station located in the office next to my secretary's desk. The principal, vice principal, and campus supervisors all had portable units tuned to the same frequency. The vice principal and I also had the capability of talking to the bus drivers and emergency vehicles as well as the district office. In a day and age where the administrators are spread very thin and expected to be everywhere at once, such a system allows constant coordinated communication. It is also very useful when the phone system is not functioning, such as during a major earthquake or storm.

Meanwhile the office staff, having heard the radio exchange on the office radio, immediately pulled the student's emergency card and my secretary radioed me that she had it ready. Having my hands full with the crowd control of the students who wanted to see what was happening, I asked her to call the parents and inform them that their child was injured and would soon be on the way to the hospital emergency room. I asked her to have them meet the ambulance there.

As soon as the ambulance left the scene, the vice principal and I ushered the students back to class and I made an announcement on the all-call explaining who was hurt and what was being done and promised to keep them informed as to the condition of the young man. I felt that it was important to do this to prevent rumors from starting and students from calling the hospital.

Remember, it is very frustrating for the teachers who are trapped in their rooms during an emergency and do not know what is happening. It is even more irritating when some of their students seem to know more about what is going on than they do. They are stuck fielding questions from the students and attempting to make sense out of a situation while they are hearing rumors, stories, and concern from the students and nothing from the administration. I always attempted to keep the staff fully informed about anything going on that was out of the ordinary.

At that point, I only knew who was hurt and that it was very serious. I confirmed that my secretary had contacted the parents and then called my superintendent, informing her of the incident and what I was doing. I then went to the hospital to check on the student and his family.

The doctor informed the parents and me that the boy was not expected to live. After consoling the parents and making sure that they were being cared for, I went back to the school. I made an announcement at the end of the last period to the students that their friend was in extremely serious condition. I asked them to not go to the hospital and told them that I would keep them informed and then I announced a faculty meeting immediately following school.

Before the announcement, my vice principal and counselor met with me to discuss how we should proceed in the event of the boy's death. The counselor suggested that I call Grief Busters, a local counseling group, and ask for advice. At the faculty meeting, I informed everyone about all we knew and told them what we would do in the event of the student's death. We also talked about discussions that should be held with the student body during advisory period the next day. This included allowing students to voice their concerns and feelings. The counselor helped coach the teachers in how this should be done.

The boy died overnight, and the next day I proceeded as follows:

- ◆ I informed the teachers in writing through a note placed in their mailboxes about his death and wrote a statement that could be read to the students.

- ◆ A special grief room was set up in the library with counselors available for students to talk to throughout the day.

- ◆ Several large blank poster pages were placed in the grief room with felt pens available for students to write feelings on, with some pages for students to write condolences to the family. I took these posters to the boy's parents the next day and offered to help them in any way.

◆ The information for the memorial for the student was posted in every room, along with a statement that attending the memorial was an excused absence only if parents requested it.

◆ A memorial service was set for the students at the school.

◆ I remained in close contact with the parents throughout. This student was from a non-English-fluent family, and I had to help them with many of the decisions and communications.

Needless to say, the campus was in severe emotional upset for many days. There were drives to collect money to help the family pay the medical and funeral expenses. Every opportunity was made to make sure that every person was listened to. Over time the sadness left us and the campus returned to normal. I received many letters and comments about how well we attended to the sad situation. I spent many hours writing in my journal about what we did, what worked, what did not, and how I would proceed in the future in the event of another trauma like this one. With over 900 students and staff members, it was bound to happen again.

DEATH OF A KEY STAFF MEMBER

The death of any person in the school community is difficult at best. Many administrators, unfortunately, have had to deal with death in their schools, usually with student death. Most school districts have developed procedures for schools to follow when there is a suicide, serious disease, drive-by shooting, or gang conflict resulting in the death of a student, but these procedures rarely help the site administrator when he or she first encounters a fatal situation.

One situation that most districts prepare for is the death of a staff member. What happens when one of your staff members dies or is killed? If there is a long-term illness, members of the school community can prepare for the death or at least understand how it happened. Sometimes, however, death comes quickly and without warning, as illustrated by the following story from Bill Sommers, principal of South High in Minneapolis.

On the Monday of the second week of school, two staff members came to me wondering where one of my assistant principals was because they had been looking for her. I found out that she had not arrived at school yet and assumed that she was late for some simple reason such as traffic or something forgotten causing her to return home. In any event I knew that she would have a good reason since she was so dependable. As time went on and she was still not there and not answering her phone at home, I became more and more concerned. Two staff members asked to go look for her.

The teachers went to her home and found her dead in her bedroom. We found out later that the death was caused by complications from diabetes. The death of a staff member was a problem I had never experienced or was trained to handle!

Fortunately, I already had a crisis team in place and I immediately called the team together to discuss how to tell the staff and students. We decided to hold meetings during lunch periods to notify the staff first. After the staff was notified, we then made announcements over the public address system followed by the staff conducting question-and-answer sessions in their rooms. Any staff member who needed a counselor or a support person received help in their classroom. Supervisors were called, counselors were brought in, and a plan was developed for the school community. This was similar to the crisis plan already established.

In addition to the procedures developed, other issues needed to be resolved. A liaison with the family and staff was established to coordinate information and provide support. Colleagues throughout the school system were contacted through a network set up for just this purpose. A memorial service to be held in 4 days was organized in school for students and staff who would not be able to attend the funeral services. It is extremely important that the school community be able to reach some closure when the death of staff occurs. This required assistance from other school administrators. We all know that school does not stop just because this kind of a crisis happens.

While the funeral services were being planned, we prepared the memorial service to be held during school time. Representatives from the school board, system administrators, church, community, staff, students, and business partners were invited to speak. The most difficult part of preparing for this was the short time I had for planning. This is why I had to reach out for additional help. A colleague, Dr. Willarene Beasley, from another school was the primary resource who helped me through this crisis. Keep in mind that seating, staging, programs, flowers, and all the other details need to be seen to in a very short period of time.

The students demonstrated leadership and great behavior even though the service lasted longer than a normal school day. We held the buses to allow students to attend the entire service. In short, dealing effectively with this kind of crisis requires many committed people working long hours. You cannot do it yourself.

SCARCITY AND PRIORITIZING

Making do is the motto for the modern-day principal. It seems that there is never enough money to do anything the way we want to. I remember seeing a water leak coming out from underneath a portable building. I watched as the maintenance man took the skirt off, revealing a drainpipe from a sink connected to the sewer pipe, about 12 inches away, by a waxed cardboard trough suspended by wires. Obviously, the "repair" had been made years ago when no money was available for maintenance. The year before I left the middle school, I had a preventive maintenance budget of $100. When I complained that it was too little to do anything with, it was removed completely.

During hard times, morale can suffer if teachers and other staff members perceive that others are getting more than they are. Both of us worked in our schools to increase trust and deal with scarcity by sharing information with the staff about the budget and involving them in decision making on most monetary decisions. Margaret Wheatley, author of *Leadership and the New Science* (1992) and, with Myron Kellner-Rogers, *A Simpler Way* (1996), says that everyone should have access to any information needed to make a decision. To build trust and run our schools more efficiently, we provided department chairs with all of the budget information. South High also provided the teachers with all of the staffing information, against the recommendation of some of the administrative team.

As a result, for the first time the teachers came to realize just how little money we were talking about. With this knowledge and understanding, some department chairs were willing to shift money from their budgets to other departments so they could make major purchases, and then the next year departments that received extra money were willing to help those who shared.

Sooner or later, every principal will deal with the problem of the old copy machine. Copy machines are very expensive to run and to repair. Teachers seem to think that they should have a right to make unlimited copies, but the truth is someone has to pay. At New Brighton Middle School, I gave the teachers all of the copy budget money, divided into each teacher's budget. They could choose to spend their money for anything that they needed, including copies. I saw to it that the copy machine ran as a no-profit program. They also found out that once the duplicating costs are subtracted, there was not very much money to operate their classes or the school. This stopped rumors of the principal stockpiling money.

Both of us, as principals, reserved some money, about 10%, for our options or emergencies that cannot be predicted. The teachers were also informed of this. Opening the budget took away a major cause for suspicion from the staff.

I also opened the budget and staffing to my site council. Once the information was open, trust increased, the reality of tough decisions was understood, and creative problem solving began.

When dealing with staffing, people wanted input but did not want to be responsible for cutting jobs. Since I was responsible, I retained the final say on what position would be changed. Since we are in a time where many people are retiring, cutting people may not be the problem, but cutting positions or departments is. I used a part of Roger Fisher and William Ury's process from their book *Getting to YES* (1981) to help. What objective measures are we using as a standard? Student enrollment obviously became the easiest. When I got there, positions had people's name on them. No longer could we afford to just replace retirements without considering student and parent requests.

6

Mediating Conflict

When I first began teaching, my principal held a staff development meeting. The point of the training was that if we want people to learn quickly, we need to raise the level of stress in the learner. As I remember, the quote was, "Stress is the best teacher." The presenter never was able to finish the presentation because of the reaction from the teachers. We knew from experience that if people are ever to be truly receptive to learning they must be in a stress-free state of mind.

As the years went on and I learned more about learning, I also discovered that people learn best in a relaxed atmosphere while they are reflecting with another person.

Knowing this led me to a process for pursuing excellence in my profession, the profession of teaching and administrating. That process is called *peer coaching*. A coach is someone who helps us succeed in an area we want to succeed. We all have situations where we could use a good coach to improve a skill or think about an idea. Even the best of us needs a coach—Tiger Woods has a coach—but the coaching we are talking about is quite different from most coaching concepts. The form of coaching Bill and I use is Cognitive Coaching©.

In Cognitive Coaching©, the coach mediates the thinking of the person being coached. Even though we are all, at the same time, an individual and a part of something else, teachers usually see themselves as alone and without support. Professionally they usually prefer to remain in the "one-room schoolhouse" within their school. Rarely do teachers seek solutions for professional problems from their peers. Mediative coaching can prepare people for those times when they are confronted by problems and are away from instant help. Teachers are prepared through interactive coaching sessions to meet potential trouble by thinking through anticipated problems and developing a framework for self-coaching when the need arises. When a staff becomes skilled in coaching techniques, they can help each other as the needs arise.

Cognitive Coaching© is a peer-coaching method developed by Art Costa and Bob Garmston from California. In the process, a coach mediates the thinking of the teacher. The term *mediate* is defined in the book *Cognitive Coaching: A Foundation for Renaissance Schools* (1994), by Costa and Garmston.

What do we mean by mediate? A mediator is one who:

Diagnoses and envisions desired stages for others

Constructs and uses clear and precise language in the facilitation of others' cognitive development

Devises an overall strategy through which individuals will move themselves toward desired states

Maintains faith in the potential for continued movement toward more holonomous states of mind and behavior

Possesses a belief in his/her own capacity to serve as an empowering catalyst of another's growth

Because the coaches are mediators, they are freed from having to be "experts" for the people they coach. Once a person is skilled in Cognitive Coaching©, he or she can coach anyone in anything. Cognitive Coaches do not provide expert advice in the coaching process.

COGNITIVE COACHING© — PLANNING AND REFLECTING

Learning conversations based on Cognitive Coaching© fall into one of two types: planning or reflecting.

Planning

In a planning conference, the coach is trying to help a teacher be specific about goals for an upcoming event, describe what success will look like in as much detail as possible, discuss how students will achieve the goals or outcomes, and finally decide what students are personally learning. The more specifically a teacher can describe to the coach each of the above parts, the better chance the teacher has of having a successful lesson.

Briefly, the Cognitive Coach assists teachers in planning and teaching a lesson by helping the teachers establish in their mind the

- ◆ Goals and outcomes for the lesson
- ◆ Method of assessing the success of the lesson
- ◆ Teaching method or methods to be used
- ◆ Personal growth focus for the teacher

This conference is usually done face-to-face between the teacher and the coach. When it is completed, the teacher usually writes a lesson plan and then teaches the lesson with an eye on the results of the planning conference. The teacher may or may not have the coach present in the room while the lesson is being taught, but the teacher knows that after the lesson he or she and the coach will meet to reflect on the results.

Reflecting

Judy Arin-Krupp said at a 1987 workshop, "Adults do not learn from the event, they learn from processing the event." I wholeheartedly agree. Every time I have engaged staff members in a reflective dialogue, they have gained new insights, developed a new plan for the next time they teach, and increased their competence and confidence as a teacher. I think this is one of the best outcomes of coaching each other. There is a sense of ownership and autonomy and, at the same time, a sense of interdependence. We can discuss our practice, gain knowledge and precision, and not be in an evaluative situation, which sometimes is threatening. W. Edwards Deming said, "Drive fear out of the organization." Having reflective conversations decreases fear and increases learning.

As we become conscious of the ability to plan and reflect prior to and after the event, there is an increase in reflection-in-action. Donald Schön (1983) writes about that process. He describes this as being able to reflect while doing the task. Teachers do that all the time.

Principals do that all the time. The question is how do we get better at reflecting while in the midst of an event?

Actually, we already do this to some extent. Have you ever said inside your head, "This isn't working"? You are reflecting in-action. One way to get better is to talk about it with a critical friend. Another way is to journal or use metacognitive strategies. Anything that will increase your consciousness about your thinking and what goes on inside your head will cause more reflection. Once you are more aware of your thoughts, you are able to monitor those thoughts and make better decisions.

Reflection begins after the lesson is taught. The coach again assists the teacher in reflecting on what was taught in relation to the points established during the planning conference. At this time the coach asks the teacher,

◆ To summarize his or her impressions of the lesson

◆ To recall data to support those impressions

Then the coach guides the teacher in establishing cause-and-effect relationships between his or her actions as a teacher and student results.

The relationships between teacher behavior and student results are filed away in the teacher's memory for future use when the coach is not present, because in the classroom the teacher cannot call "time out" and suspend the students' actions while he or she goes to the sideline to consult an ever-present coach.

A teacher must rely on stored knowledge of what works throughout the day, whether in planning, teaching, or reflecting. Although the coaching process is best done with a separate coach over time, a teacher who is experienced with the process of Cognitive Coaching© can self-coach when a physical coach is not available.

It is not our intention to provide complete and effective instruction to the reader about Cognitive Coaching© in this book. The descriptions given here are to provide an overall feeling for the process. We recommend that co-coaches take training in the process Cognitive Coaching© from the Center for Cognitive Coaching in Denver, Colorado.

INTRODUCING COGNITIVE COACHING©
IN THE SCHOOL

There are many ways for a principal to work from the top down. A leader can lead by decree, but this rarely establishes long-term results. A staff that does not buy into a decree will find ways to "go through the motions" while the principal is present and ignore the decree when he or she walks out the door. As soon as the "law behind the decree" leaves, the staff usually reverts to old habits.

An effective leader can lead by example if he or she is respected. This can work when a new principal steps into a job if the principal has a successful reputation. If the staff believes that the new leader is an expert or trusts the leader's experience, he or she will be able to be effective with some top-down programs.

Another effective way that a leader can work is from behind by urging the staff to move ahead through suggestion, coaching, and staff development. The staff moves in the direction the leader wishes to go because they feel listened to, involved in the decision, and respected. They move out of respect and learning, not because of fear. As the old cowboy says, "If the goal is to get the herd across the creek, who cares where each cow crosses!"

This is a constructivist view of leadership. It allows each teacher to build his or her own belief that the direction of movement is the right one. The following is an example of how I introduced coaching to my middle school:

It was the first day of school for the teachers— one of those late August hot days, the first day back from the summer break. The teachers arrived in ones, twos, and threes. Excitement was high, with plans and ideas for the new school year. I had sent a letter out over the summer asking the riddle, "How is a great middle school like a Cajun music festival?" Many of the teachers were puzzled and asking for the answer.

We met in a classroom, and as the teachers entered I asked them to find their seats. The room was already set up with three chairs around each table and each table held three high-quality blank journals on it together with three pens. Each journal had the name of the teacher assigned to it on the cover. (More about journals later.) I had deliberately placed the teachers in triad groups to prepare them to coach each other in the process of planning and reflecting about their teaching. The members of each triad were carefully chosen to encourage a strong relationship within the team and prevent saboteurs from poisoning the beginning of a new idea. In fact, I placed my three most negative staff members in one triad. That way only one triad would be affected and not three.

After welcoming the teachers, I asked for the results of the riddle. "Any ideas?"

One person responded that since we were dealing with middle school children maybe I meant "Cageum!" After several other attempts, I explained that I had attended a Cajun music festival that summer and, at one point during the music, I noticed that each member of the band was playing a different instrument. I also noticed that they were all pulsing up and down together, moving in harmony to the beat of the music. I looked at the hundreds of people in that green field on that beautiful summer day, listening and dancing to the exciting music, and I saw that they were all pulsing up and down precisely with the beat of the music.

At that moment, I began to think about New Brighton Middle School and realized that all of the teachers had different styles and skills, yet the entire school danced to the same beat. They all had the same concept of what our middle school was: Teachers, administrators, parents, students, and community all knew the "beat" and danced with it. What a beautiful realization that was—that after 4 years we were so together! I wanted to ensure that we could continue to "dance well to the music" to the benefit of our students for years to come.

At that point, I turned on a tape player with a Cajun music tape and music filled the room. It was captivating, and soon many of the teachers were up and dancing. Everyone was moving together to the beat.

I was working on the state of *holonomy* with my staff. According to Costa and Garmston in their book *Cognitive Coaching: A Foundation for Renaissance Schools* (1994), the word *holonomy* comes "from the Greek: *holos* meaning whole and *on* meaing part" (p. 130). In other words, we exist simultaneously as a single entity and as a part of something bigger.

The concept holonomy is extremely important to a successful school. Traditionally, teachers work alone in classrooms with their students and rarely talk or read professionally. It has been said that the one-room schoolhouse is repeated room by room down the halls of our schools. The staff room is rarely a place to exchange professional ideas; rather it is a place for time out or chatting. The faculty meeting is usually "something to get over and done with so that I can get back to my room." Staff development is usually looked on as "something to get over and done with so that I can get back to my room."

It is important for members of a learning organization to interact with each other. Schools have often been places where this is not a natural state of mind. I feel that a school should be a place where teachers are both independent and interdependent professionally. From the first day, I began to work on ways for teachers to develop a holonomous feeling. When I placed the entire staff in triads, I was making a major advance in developing holonomy. When I determined the makeup of the triads, I gambled on the fact that I had respect and trust from my staff because they knew that sooner or later they would have effective input to anything new that I did. The gamble paid off.

The triads in my school were established to allow Cognitive Coaching© to take place. Because the process of Cognitive Coaching© allows people to help other people think deeply about something, I chose to make it a habit of mind in my school. In this case, I wanted my teachers to coach each other in the process of teaching. The triads had a second purpose. Each team was composed of one teacher from each grade level—6, 7, and 8—so that there would be vertical interaction. I had discovered that the main interaction on the staff professionally was horizontal, sixth-grade teachers talking to sixth-grade teachers and so on.

I asked the teachers to please bear with me and excuse the extremely top down nature of this request and to try my experiment with coaching for 1 year. I promised them that at the end of the year they would help determine the value of coaching and decide if it was to continue.

Near the end of the year, I gave the teachers a large part of a faculty meeting and told them that they were to discuss the merits of coaching and decide whether or not we should continue the process in the next school year. I also asked them to recommend any changes if they decided to keep it. Then, after turning the meeting over to a teacher, I walked out and back to my office.

I sat in my office eagerly awaiting their decision. I was almost certain that they would vote it out, but to my surprise they unanimously chose to continue the program in the following year. They requested that we change from the vertical grouping of sixth to eighth grade to horizontal groups by grade level and job.

Finding time for anything "extra" in schools is always a problem. To clear time and space for the coaching project without adding extra teacher workday time took some thinking. I felt that if I were to ask them to add this project on top of their already-busy schedules without providing the time for it out of our school day it would kill the program before it started. I discovered that the school board had a regulation stating that all teachers must be in their classrooms with the classroom open 30 minutes before school started. Teachers were not allowed to do anything other than be available for students during that time. I went to the school board and asked if I could have half of the teachers excused from this rule every Wednesday for the purpose of coaching. They agreed to the proposal and we were on our way.

Every Wednesday, half of the triads would meet, for the purpose of coaching, in the morning before school. During that time, the other half of the teachers had their rooms open and the administration helped supervise the remaining campus beyond our usual patrolling. Each triad could meet twice each month under this arrangement. I would have loved more time, but it was a beginning.

One of the requirements, I stated, was that each triad provide me with minutes from its meeting. The reason for this was to guarantee that the purpose of the meeting was being adhered to. I kept these notes in a folder and did not bother to read many of them. Here again there was a risk of breaking trust, but the staff expressed to me many times that it was good to have to provide notes to keep the group on task. The very fact that the notes were taken seemed to guarantee that the meeting was sincere and purposeful. Each Wednesday I confirmed the fact that the groups were seriously working by walking into sessions and listening.

Along with the triad meetings, I paid for substitutes on days when teachers in the triads wanted to watch each other teach. Most of the teachers availed themselves of this opportunity, although I did not force it.

The overall benefit of the program is difficult to overstate. The teachers were now talking about their profession. They were actively discussing successes and problems. More important, they were looking at what they did to make something successful; they were discovering the evidence that let them self-determine that a particular lesson or action worked. On the other hand, when something did not work they focused first on the evidence that let them know that something was not working and then reflected on how they might do it differently in the future utilizing what they had learned from the past.

I do not mean to make it sound as if every teacher was participating with full heart and soul in the process. As an educator, you realize that it is impossible to bring every staff member along on a project. It is also true that not every triad was successful. I would be willing to state, however, that every teacher did, more than once, have a professional conversation about his or her teaching. Not many schools can claim that.

The real power of coaching comes when staff members coach each other. I cannot coach everyone in the building. Bill Sommers reports that while he was at Wayzata High School, staff learning increased when teachers started coaching each other. He trained the secretarial staff in some linguistic skills to better handle their jobs when dealing with students, teachers, or parents. His secretary often coached him before he would go to a meeting, evaluate a staff member, or teach a lesson. Bill tells the following story to illustrate his way of working:

It was the last day of the quarter, a grading day with no students. It was the day before Thanksgiving vacation and the teachers who had turned in their grades were excused at noon. At 12:30 PM a parent met me as I was leaving my office. He had just berated my receptionist for something that I did not completely hear. As he entered my office, I retreated to my chair and offered him one. He refused the chair and stood in front of me telling me that his daughter always got As and that one of my teachers had given her a C grade! Then he told me that he wanted me to change the C to an A and do it *now!*

I informed him that I was not going to change the grade that a teacher gave a student and asked him to give me more information. He then moved to challenging me. "Don't you have the authority to change a grade?"

I said, yes, but I was not going to do so without the teacher being present and that teacher was on his way to Arkansas to visit his family. The father started yelling and threatening to take this to the school board. I used my usual response strategies to reduce his anger. He finally left, unhappy but not yelling or threatening.

I started breathing again and in walked my receptionist. She asked, "How did you do that?"

I responded, "Do what?"

She said that he was off the wall when he came in but left at least not yelling. I said that I have response strategies by my phone and on the wall next to the door jamb. I told her some of the techniques.

She asked, "Will you teach me to use them?"

I had never thought about sharing those strategies with the secretarial group and I said I would if she would ask the others if they would be interested. We set up three 1 1/2-hour workshops after school during the next month. Eleven out 12 clerical staff members attended. Forty-five minutes was school time and 45 minutes was their time.

Since the majority of communication is nonverbal and the clerical staff spends a lot of time on the phone, it seemed so natural, I wished I had thought of the idea. I did the same at my next two schools to teach those who have to deal with angry people to build their capacity. I named this project the "Hazel Smith Response Strategy School" after Hazel Smith, my receptionist.

Coaching can work on anybody with a willing attitude. I coached a custodian at a junior high where I was principal. I had taken an assignment as a junior high principal as a 1-year replacement for a person on sabbatical. I only knew the principal's secretary, the head custodian, and one teacher. When I met the staff in the fall I talked about the coaching I was doing and told them that I would be looking for volunteers. One staff member asked if he could find out more about coaching, so I set up an hour meeting to explain the process to anyone who was interested. About 15 staff members showed up and to my surprise the head custodian, Bob Wagner, came along with them.

As we coached each other that year, he examined his management style, his relationship with the building and grounds director, and some issues he had with the teaching staff. In the spring of the year, after one of our conversations, I asked Bob why he had volunteered.

He said, "I have had the reputation as a hothead. I get really mad when teachers don't respect my need for their cooperation. I was hoping to maybe change some of my attitudes." I responded by asking how he would know if anything had changed. As a result, Bob sent out a survey that spring. To his credit, he received great feedback that matched what I was hearing informally from the staff. The staff said that they were impressed that Bob would volunteer to be coached, they felt he was easier to talk to since the coaching began, and work they requested was completed quickly. They also stated that he was a more pleasant person to work with.

When we had our final conversation before I returned to my job at the high school, he was feeling very positive about the experience and so were the teachers. I had discovered that coaching was for everyone, not just teachers in the classroom. Since that time I have always offered coaching workshops to support staff as well as the certified staff.

TRUST AND YOUR PARTNER

I heard somewhere that trust is a two-part process that includes being trusting and trustworthy. To enter a coaching situation, each member of the team must have trust in the others and, at the same time, be trusted by the others. This requires confidence that what is discussed does not end up as general conversation in the teachers' room or some other public place. To ensure a trusting atmosphere is maintained, each coaching team member must be skilled in the process. This requires that each member follow the agreed-on rules for coaching, which include

◆ Remember that the purpose is to help the other person think and not for the coach to provide information to the teacher being coached. This is because teachers spend much of the time working alone with children and must learn to think for themselves most of the time.

- ◆ Avoid criticizing each other's work with either praise or negative comments, because it is known that praise inhibits thinking.
- ◆ Refrain from offering suggestions during the process.
- ◆ Refrain from including presuppositions in questions, because presuppositions are just another way of telling.
- ◆ Allow time for people to think.

MENTAL MODELS AND MIND-SET

Principals are constantly "walking into situations" that challenge their ability to keep a school running smoothly. They have to think on their feet and be able to make decisions quickly as the day moves along. Principals' decisions are based on the beliefs they hold about schools, families, people, and life. These beliefs and the methods principals use to work within them are held as mental models. When they encounter a problem, they immediately sort through the models in their minds for solutions.

The models form maps in our minds that represent what we understand and believe about life. There are also maps about how we have successfully approached a difficult situation in the past. They have been described as templates, organizing principles, cognitive maps, and mental models. Models drive our behaviors in practice and also drive the behaviors of others we interact with.

For example, if I have the belief that parents cannot help me and only get in the way, then every parent I see becomes a problem. This mental model will cause me to find ways to keep parents out of the school as far as making any meaningful contribution. Sooner or later the parents will feel the attitude and react in a way that will only support my belief.

An established conflict between educators comes from the mental model some hold that "girls can't learn math as well as boys." If some female students are not doing well, the math teacher often will provide less challenging work, believing that they cannot do the work of boys. As the girls fall further behind, the attitude can become a self-fulfilling prophecy.

Another example is that some educators function with the mental model that a student is a vessel to fill with knowledge. They believe that there is knowledge stored in the teacher's head and that knowledge must be put into the student's head. This practice drives certain teaching methods, such as students copying notes and sitting passively listening to the teacher lecture, followed by tests about the lectures.

On the other hand, if teachers believe that students construct knowledge, then they will look at ways to scaffold the learning to help students build their own knowledge, understanding, and applications through the guidance of the teacher. They will stress constructivist teaching methods.

Similarly, when we encounter a difficult situation or problem we sort through the maps that we hold in our heads until we come to one that fits the situation. It is usually one that we have used before, but it can be one we have heard about. For example, when I encounter a group unwilling to change, I immediately begin to use strategies that have resulted in positive outcomes in the past. (See examples of change process, Cognitive Coaching©, and consensus building in previous chapters.) These immediately come to my mind from mental models of strategies that have worked.

Bill Sommers has reminders of mental models that he uses when encountering difficult problems posted by the telephone in his office. When he hears a problem, he scans the list for a template he may use to approach the situation (see Chapter 7).

The templates we use are not set in stone. We are constantly adjusting them or replacing them with other templates through experience. We can develop our own over time or learn them from workshops, books, and other people.

Changing a mental model we hold requires a willingness to change as well as proof that change is necessary. A final requirement for changing a mind-set is to have something with which to replace the old model. Coaching facilitates the examination of models in the mind and comparing them with new models. For the administrator to change another person's model requires long, hard work (see Chapter 3).

Mental models are the way we hold theories that guide our behaviors. Leadership and organizational development books are filled with constructs, mental models, and templates to guide practice.

Here is a good journal exercise:

Examine the mental models you hold. What are they? Specifically think about how you have used them in the past. How well have they worked? How do you know? In other words, what is the evidence that each model works well? Now make three lists of the models you have examined. Label one list "Mental Models That Work Well for Me," the next, "Mental Models That I Am Not Sure Of," and finally, "Mental Models That Don't Work For Me."

Attend to the second column by keeping it in mind as you use items from it. Make subtle changes in the models to see if you can make them work. What evidence would you need to indicate that they are working better?

Then look at the third column. Ask yourself, "Where can I investigate models to replace the ones that are not working?" Ask colleagues how they deal with the models you are struggling with. Do the research and try again.

TIME TO COACH

As Michael Fullan (1993) has written, three barriers continue to plague us in schools: **overload, incoherence,** and **fragmentation.** One of the major overload considerations in public education is that of time. Teachers have heavy demands on their time that cannot be interrupted easily. Aside from teaching lessons and supervising student activities, teachers have only approximately a half hour before school and an hour after school. By freeing up time during the school day, some of the overload pressure is reduced. Perhaps in the future school districts will realize that teachers need more professional time, perhaps with longer contracts, thus relieving some of the time crunch that is not felt as much in the business world.

Time is a major barrier to completing a thorough planning or reflecting conference. One solution to the time problem occurred at South High School. Bill Sommers helped start a reflective practice program with 25% of the staff voluntarily signing up for a program in which teachers and other staff members would reflect on the progress of what they were providing for each student. The staff members met off site for 2 hours, once a month after school. The teachers were provided with 1 hour from school time and the teacher donated the other hour. At each meeting one or two people would take responsibility for a presentation or activity during the first hour and the other hour would be spent reflecting on what was learned and how the school was functioning.

Everyone took some responsibility for the meeting, including providing food, finding and reserving a meeting site, sending out invitations, designing a feedback activity, and planning future meetings. Once a week, the participants would meet in dyads or triads for 1 hour to talk about how the week was proceeding. Each member was provided with a journal to be used for reflection. All the participants were encouraged to write about their reflections in the journal. About half the people wrote in the journals whereas others preferred to use their computers. During the first year, many issues surfaced and resulted in more shared responsibility for approaching problems in the school. The program is still in effect 4 years after Bill left the school.

Coaching conversations were initially designed to use with teachers, but I have successfully used my coaching skill with parents, students, and community members who were unaware of what I was doing. As administrators, we both use these processes constantly with teachers, students, other staff members, parents, and fellow administrators. I have used my coaching skills for conducting large group meetings and committee work. I have too often been a member of unproductive and time-wasting committees. I find that we can reduce time and energy by setting specific goals, developing strategies to attain those goals, and determining evidence to collect to tell us whether or not we are meeting our outcomes. This process is accomplished by asking the group coaching style questions. Bill and I have found that this works with individuals or groups equally well. Our skills as Cognitive Coaches help us accomplish successful group facilitation.

WORKING WITH PARENTS

When meeting with parents, we usually talk about *what we want to happen* (planning) or *what did happen* (reflecting) to a student or group of students. Having coaching questions in my mind helps me to direct conferences to specific goals. This helps reduce time in unproductive parent meetings and increases the specificity of action plans. Both are desirable outcomes.

7

Standing Your Ground
(Even in Quicksand)

Early in my administrative career, a seasoned teacher caught me alone in my office. It was my first year as principal of New Brighton Middle School and I was trying to avoid making a difficult decision. The teacher was waiting for me to make the decision because it affected her directly. Now, after I had spent several days of looking for a solution that would not hurt anyone's feelings, she was in my face again.

This time she said, "David, you have got to understand that you must make a decision, and until you do, I am going to make your life hell!"

At that moment I told her that the decision was "No!" She could not do what she wanted to do.

With that she stood up, hugged me, and said, "Thank you. You have saved energy for both of us." And she walked out.

Sooner or later, we have to exert the power of the office. The administrator is ultimately responsible for everything on the campus and he or she must understand that he or she cannot please everyone. Principals can, however, make their feelings known without breaking trust and still be able to maintain good relationships with those disappointed by the decision.

Most administrators started as teachers. Teachers are trained to forgive, be gentle, not hurt feelings, and say no only when they have run out of other ideas. They want to be loved, and the word *no* seems to be such a difficult one for us to say, especially to adults. Teachers do not like to make decisions that reflect on other adults, especially if those decisions may make a colleague angry.

Recently, a group of teachers asked me how to deal with objectionable people during a meeting. I said that they should tell such people what they are doing that bothers them and then ask them to stop that behavior. All of these teachers responded that they could never do that.

So there you are with your best teacher, the one you respect the most, and she has just asked for your permission to show a rented videotape to her class as a reward for selling the most candy in the candy sales for the student body fund. And, oh by the way, the film is rated "R" but only for one tiny scene that all the kids know about anyway and the topic of the film has absolutely nothing to do with her class.

The answer is obviously "No!" So why is it so hard to say? If another teacher had asked the question, one that you do not like as well or preferably one who dislikes you openly, you could easily say, "Of course not! A film like that has no business in a public school room." But it is never that easy. There she stands and you have to say no.

Unfortunately, it is your job to make these decisions—it is why you were hired. Also, if the answer would be no for the teacher you dislike, it should also be no for your all-star. It is also important for you to remain a model by holding your temper and responding in a polite and respectful way to all requests no matter who is asking.

HOW AND WHEN TO SAY NO

We are people who rise to the rank of boss from the classroom and that makes it hard for many of us to make unpopular decisions. I, for one, found it very difficult to say no to another adult, mostly because I expected adults to take responsibility for what they do, think things out, and generally not behave like their students. Silly me! It only took me a little while and a few ridiculous requests to make it clear to me that some adults need full-time supervision.

My basic philosophy for working with adults is if you treat them as adults they will act like adults. This philosophy works most of the time, but there are those who always need close supervision because they continue to make poor decisions on their own. Even when the bulk of your staff are making good decisions, there are times when you have to say no because of one reason or another. My big surprises always came from the small group of adults who never got it. My wife says, "One third of us survive because two thirds of us watch out for the one third." It is our job to try to get that one third to step up to the plate and take care of themselves.

First, there were the sudden cases of sick parents and family problems that always happened the day before a staff development day with mandatory attendance. These same staff members expressed their need to miss the training because of their need to attend to personal emergencies, of course. Missing the training just happened to give them a long weekend. Checking attendance files, I discovered that one of the teachers always had this problem. On one occasion when she asked to miss a Friday staff development meeting for health reasons, I found out that she was booked on a flight to Florida and would not to return for a week.

And then there was the teacher who informed me that she had a child care problem on teacher meeting days and asked if she could bring her "well-behaved" child to the meetings. I, being the progressive educator that I was, immediately said, "Sure!" Well, the child was very young and very cranky, crying most of the time, and the teacher had to go get her before every meeting. She would arrive after the meeting started with playpen, toys, child, and noise, disrupting the meeting. She would miss the first part of the meeting and destroy the second. It did not take too many of these incidents before I had to say no to her. It seemed easy that time!

There were many other examples, from the habitual moving to another apartment to "Can I paint my room orange?" "May I knock a hole in the wall into the adjacent teacher's room for a door so we can work together?" "Can I bring my dog to school so that she doesn't get lonely?" NO!

Perhaps the best example of indecision on my part happened during my first few weeks as principal at the middle school. The previous principal told me that the school had a program for advanced English taught by a teacher with long tenure who was very popular with the parents. He went on to state that the main problem was that the teacher was very selective about the students she allowed to be in the class. No matter who was assigned by the counselor, she would keep the ones she liked and find a way to run all of the others out. It was, in other words, a very exclusive program. She reminded me of the teacher in the movie *The Prime of Miss Jean Brody*, who was also very selective about her girls.

The previous principal volunteered to cancel the class on his watch so that I would not have to take the heat. He said, "Trust me, it will be better for you if I make the cut." I told him that if it was to be canceled, and it sounded as if it should, then I should do it. I did not want to pass the buck back to him. I allowed it to continue for one more year to observe for myself what was going on. Sure enough, it was everything the principal had told me and indeed it needed to be canceled.

As the spring approached and the new schedule was being put together, the teacher, knowing my thinking, lobbied heavily for the program and I, fearing faculty backlash and parental fury, kept putting off the decision, hoping God would strike it down or an earthquake would somehow help me out.

The results are described at the opening of this chapter. I made the decision and I did suffer the ire of the parents and some of the staff, but I lived through it and was still there 6 years later. She was not.

There are many reasons for saying no. Some of these include requests that cut across your values, such as the math teachers who wanted to go back to a math lab system that did not work. Other questions may call for extensive construction expenses that the teacher does not understand that we cannot afford. The request to put a door in a wall between two classrooms would have cost more than my budget allowed because of the need for a header and moving electrical wiring and plumbing, not to mention the cost of the door.

We get requests all day long and some come at the busiest times. We often have to answer without time to think, and use the word "no" inappropriately.

Using the Word "No!"   Box 7.1

♦ Never use no just to get rid of someone. Most requests can be granted and should be; doing so makes saying no seem more reasonable when you must.

♦ When no is the correct response, say it quickly without "weasel" words. I usually would say, "No, I can't allow that and here are my reasons . . . "

◆ When first hit by the question, say to yourself, "Why should or shouldn't I allow this?" It allows you a moment to give the request consideration.

◆ If the request comes at a bad time and seems involved and complex, or if it could be costly, I usually asked the person to put it in writing or schedule an appointment to see me at a more appropriate time. Another way of giving yourself time is to tell the person that you will get back to him or her. Be sure you do. I usually took a 3-by-5-inch card out of my pocket and wrote it down, one item per card—writing it down demonstrates that you are serious. At a quiet time, I took the cards out of my pocket, arranged them in priority piles, and then attempted to deal with them. Once I made the decision, I would immediately write a quick response and put it in the teacher's mailbox or go see him or her personally.

◆ Things to consider when making a decision include *practicality, school mission and goals, legality, money, need,* and *curriculum.*

◆ Choose your battles carefully. You could lose in the long run if you do not consider requests thoroughly.

REPRIMANDING A POOR EMPLOYEE

As an administrator, there are times when you need to have a learning conversation to help a teacher see new ways to do something. Conversely, there are those times when you need to use the power of your position to make a quick decision or give a reprimand. Due to the crunch of time, many administrators resort to the use of the Theory X process.

Theory X infers that you believe people are basically lazy and will slack off anytime they can if they are not supervised constantly. To overcome this tendency, they must be motivated by stress, fear, and intimidation. Theory X also projects the belief that the people we supervise are not capable of making important individual decisions, do not care about their profession, and are not willing to take responsibility for their actions.

Many administrators are moving away from this belief as research shows that people work better in a cooperative atmosphere. There are, however, times when "telling" is the quickest and best way to get things done.

Admittedly, principals have responsibilities that require them to make tough decisions—decisions that produce very emotional responses from those affected. As a principal, I must watch out for the law and the education of each child. I was hired because of my vision and values and the way I fit with the vision of the school and district, but also to manage people. No matter how much shared decision making I allow, if another person or group's decision goes against our vision, values, or the law I cannot allow it. This does not mean that we support the idea that stress, fear, and intimidation are good motivators. Neither does it mean that when we make an executive decision without input that we believe members of the staff are not capable of guiding themselves.

When it comes to quick, top-down decisions without input and time is of the essence, just say what you mean quickly and pointedly. Do not try to camouflage the fact that it is your decision. As an example: "I expect everyone to be at the meeting today at 3:00 PM. I also expect everyone to be on time." Or, "I have decided to change the way we operate the copy machine budget. I have put your copy budget money in your classroom accounts and you can choose to spend your money as you wish. Be advised that copies will be charged to your account at a rate of 2 cents per copy. When your budget is gone, it is gone."

Confronting people about problems does not have to be gut wrenching or cause us to be hostile. When it comes time to tell someone to do something or to confront someone with something that is bothering us, we need to be careful not to abuse the person or strip him or her of dignity. This is done by being direct and to the point, for example, saying, "I want you to know that allowing a student to enter grades in your gradebook is not only illegal but is a dereliction of your duties. I expect you to refrain from doing it in the future and I will be putting a letter in your file to remind you of this conversation. If it happens again I will start disciplinary action."

Always be direct and to the point. Refrain from using weasel words such as, "I know that you are a very hard working teacher, however . . . " Or, "You do a lot of good things but I want to point out one . . . " Weasel words only detract from the statement. Remember, when it comes to a reprimand the person reprimanded does not want to be there and nothing you say will change the situation. In other words, make it short, direct, and to the point. Box 7.2 gives my formula for reprimanding.

Formula for Reprimanding   Box 7.2

1. You did . . .
2. It is wrong because . . .
3. Here is what I am doing about it . . .
4. If it happens again . . .
5. A follow-up file letter should be stated in the same way.

A final consideration. I have found that when I have reprimanded someone, the person will want to talk to me again within a day. As a result, I try not to give reprimands on a Friday since the reprimanded person has the weekend before he or she can talk to you again. This means that those 2 days can be completely ruined as the person attempts to resolve the problem in his or her mind without your input. There are, however, situations where the actions of the staff member are so out of line that the reprimand cannot wait until Monday.

The timeliness of a reprimand is very important. Once a principal reprimanded me and placed a letter in my file for an incident that happened 2 years earlier. He was under the gun from the superintendent to reprimand teachers and chose many of us to write up for old events. Later I was easily able to have the letter removed.

This incident was clear in my mind after I initiated a severe reprimand to a teacher. An art teacher was being transferred from teaching art to teaching another class in the fall because of program need. He was bitter about the reassignment and chose to attack me during the spring open house.

Every year, with the help of the other art teachers, he put on a show of student work and it was very popular with the parents and students. This year, however, instead of an art show he put a note on a blank display wall. The note informed all the parents that because of his transfer there would be no more art shows in the future. This was not true; there were still art classes and the other art teachers would put on the shows. In other words, he was taking his anger with me out on students by convincing the other teachers to go along with the protest. Using students that way was inexcusable in my mind.

Our new superintendent had instituted a procedure for reprimands. Before I could deliver a letter of reprimand to anyone, it had to be reviewed by the assistant superintendent. I verbally reprimanded the teacher and then delivered the follow-up letter to the assistant superintendent with a note to please address the situation ASAP. Even with reminders, I did not receive my letter back with an OK for two months. I refused to deliver it because it was too long past the incident and I felt it made us look bad in the eyes of the teacher.

MISUSE OF THEORY X

I watched the effect of stress caused by the poor use of Theory X up close and personal when one of the high school teachers I worked with was on the principal's "get rid of" list. He was a friend of mine and I knew him well. He was what I would call a "low abstract" teacher. By that I mean that he just did not see what he was doing wrong and therefore could not understand why the principal was after him. Whatever the principal said and thought, he did not communicate it clearly to the teacher. Neither did he suggest ways that the teacher could improve in a way that the teacher would understand.

The principal's goal was to put pressure on the teacher to quit. The teacher was told that if he did not "improve" he would be fired. He was not told how to improve. The proper procedure to terminate a poor teacher was not followed.

At one point during this time, I walked into the teacher's classroom during class. The students were running wild and the teacher had his feet up on a chair. He was reading a newspaper. He looked at me with a sorrowful expression and said, "Did you hear? The principal is picking on me and I don't know why. He doesn't like me and is out to get me." The teacher suffered for months but never changed a bit.

The principal eventually left his job, leaving the teacher in the classroom still doing a poor job for kids. After many more years of poor teaching, the teacher finally retired. In other words, the process did not work, and in my view the principal was derelict in his duty.

He let the poor teacher's students down by not approaching the problem correctly. He was not being specific about what he wanted from the teacher and did not provide opportunities for the teacher's professional development. Had the principal done so, he would have set up the teacher in a situation where he would have improved or could have been documented for poor performance and then fired.

All of us have our ways of working with people and most of them have been developed through experience over time. I know that I have a hammer that I can use when I need to, but I like to leave the hammer to the last resort. What follows is an example demonstrating one way I approach a problem teacher. I have learned this approach over time and it works well for me. Remember, we all have to put our own spin on others' techniques. I always attempt to work with people before I just "let them have it" and lower the boom.

When I am dealing with a problem with a teacher and a parent, I first try to establish whether the parent has a valid complaint, and if so I go directly to the teacher, knowing that pride will often prevent him or her from seeing the problem. In such a case I like to tell the teacher that in the eye of the perceiver perception is a fact. I explain that no matter what you feel about yourself you need to know that this is the perception the parent has, so how are you going to address the perception?

As an example, I had a teacher who often yelled at her class when the students acted up. This was a real yell and usually resulted in the class laughing at her. She did not want to let me know about the problem and get help. Other administrators had told her to stop yelling, and still she persisted. I approached her with the statement that it was a parent's perception that she was yelling too often in her class. She immediately wanted to know which parent. I answered that I would tell her in good time, but she needed to know that it was not the first time I had heard about the perception. I asked her what she intended to do to deal with that perception. She told me that she knew that she "occasionally" raised her voice to the class but that she did not think of it as a yell. I coached her to the point where she realized that regardless of how few times she "raised her voice," it would only confirm the perception that she yelled. She decided to investigate other ways to discipline a rowdy class. I made sure that I did follow-up visits to follow her progress and left notes of praise for her when I saw good things happening.

Another tip: When you are preparing for a battle, remember that you can either win, lose, or draw. Remember that every battle takes time, emotion, and energy. If I feel there is no chance to win, then I reevaluate the situation. I always choose my fight carefully, because if I am going to go down in flames, I would rather go down attempting to take out an aircraft carrier than a rowboat. Another benefit to this philosophy comes from the fact that because you choose your fights carefully you are not always fighting. People begin to realize that when you do take a strong stand you mean it. It causes them to think twice about a confrontation with you.

I remember a specific example of a teacher who had done something so wrong that I had to consider her dismissal. Two former principals of the school told me that she had done similar things during their tenure. They both told me that they had written her up, but when I went to her file there was only one letter from a previous principal and it was very old. I knew just how difficult it was to fire a teacher in California, but I was determined to do so. I was once told by Susan Kovalak, a longtime educator and friend, that administrators need to keep in mind how many children a bad teacher can mistreat over a career. She said that even though it is painful to dismiss a teacher, concern for the children should always come first.

To make a long story short, even though we had the teacher dead to rights our lawyer said that the judge would put her back in the classroom because she had not been sufficiently warned. I was very upset and agreed to back away from pursuing the termination only if the reprimand from the board was severe enough so that we could get rid of her the next time. In the long run, she left education. As a result of this incident, it became clear to me that every principal has the duty to children to accurately document poor teacher behavior to facilitate the termination of those people who do not belong in the classroom.

As a result of this incident, we retrained all of our administrators in the use of Mary Jo McGrath's templates for reprimand and a process for keeping a record of teacher behavior. The process is so effective that I recommend that all administrators become trained in it or a similar program (see "Teacher Evaluation," Chapter 8). We would also point out the obvious. If it ever becomes necessary to terminate an employee, you must have established a valid paper trail containing evidence of the behaviors that led to the termination and showing what the district has attempted to do to remediate the employee.

DEALING WITH DIFFICULT PEOPLE

I watched out the window as she pulled into the parking lot too fast and screeched to a stop. She vaulted out of the car and stormed toward the office looking like a storm trooper. I braced myself and announced, "Here comes Mary again, get ready." Mary (a parent—but this is not her real name) came at me at least twice a week with one complaint or another. Usually her problems were based on misinformation or she was angry with a teacher for not doing something for her child or maybe doing something to her precious child. She was almost always unreasonable. I always had a difficult time dealing with her. This time was different.

As she advanced on the office door, I noticed that her car was beginning to roll backward out of the parking lot. (It eventually crossed the street and went through a fence into the front yard of a neighbor, fortunately not hurting anyone in the process.) With her back to the car, Mary came roaring through the door, pointing her finger at me and saying, "There you are! I want to talk to you."

Before she could go on, I asked as I pointed out the window, "Is that your car?"

She turned to look, still attempting to say something, and saw the car moving out of the lot. Panic set in and she ran out the door following the car yelling, "Stop! Stop!" with her finger still pointing in the air. She did not return for over a week, and I never did discover what she had planned to attack me for on that day.

Difficult people love to go after principals and teachers. Unfortunately, you rarely have the "rolling car" solution, so what do you do when that person or group is never satisfied or reasonable?

I had a way of working with difficult people when they came into my office that worked well for me. There are usually two phases of a confrontation with these people. The *first* is the initial confrontation and the *second* is finding a way for them to back away without them losing face or you giving in completely.

To start with, my secretary usually knew when a problem person was approaching and could warn me. I would close my door and compose myself by self-coaching. I would remind myself that I had the skills to deal with this person and I would clear my desk and arrange a chair for the person, usually across a table from me. Then I would go out to the outer office, ask the person in, and request that he or she sit down in the chair indicated.

Sometimes people are too agitated to sit immediately, and in that case we would start our conversation standing. I almost always start the conversation with the statement and question, "Good morning Mr. Smith. I can see that something is troubling you. What seems to be the problem?"

With that, most people blast back. I let them talk themselves out while attempting to grasp the problem. If they yell, I tell them that I will not tolerate that in my office and say, "I am going to leave."

Once the original burst is over, I reach for a pad of paper and say something like, "Wow, I can really see that you are upset. I was not able to keep up with all the details so let me ask questions and take some notes." Then I paraphrase the first point in his statement. "I understand that this problem stems from a disagreement between your son and a teacher. Tell me some background about how you discovered this."

The meeting goes on with me paraphrasing and asking questions. Often during this phase parents discover their own solution or we find a common ground. The parent says, "We both want Jimmy to pass the seventh grade. Can we agree on a way to proceed?"

Bill Sommers' son asked a few years ago, "Dad, what do you do all day?" I responded, "I go to meetings and I try to solve conflicts." As I reflected on this answer, I thought, "Yes, that is what a principal does." I am always conferencing, meeting both individuals and groups, often dealing with conflict situations. Rarely, although it does happen, do teachers come in and tell me great things are happening in their classrooms or parents tell me how much they appreciated what a teacher or custodian had done for them.

When confronted with a problem, our first step is to avoid downshift. Brain theory tells us that when we are under stress or feeling attacked, our brain automatically takes over. Our emotional center attempts to save us by putting us into a fight or flight mode.

Being in the fight or flight mode is not conducive to calm problem solving. To solve problems, it is extremely important to be able to think and consider your options. This is not possible when the brain has been hijacked and you are feeling attacked. This process worked well for us when we were threatened by tigers and lions, but we must learn to override the emotional hijacker and continue to think clearly.

When I encounter a situation that sets off an emotional response, I begin to control my emotional reflexes by controlling my breathing.

I start to breathe low in my diaphragm. I have found that it is necessary to get as much oxygen to the brain as possible to think more clearly in those near-panic situations. If I get trapped on the phone with someone who is angry, I stand up and start to move. It helps me to become more relaxed to be in motion rather than sitting frozen in panic.

Firefighters and ambulance drivers have to practice and practice emergency routines to imprint them on their brains. If they could not easily find the mental maps for responding to a dangerous or gory situation, the fight or flight syndrome would most likely overcome them. In that mode, they would be of no use to the people who need them.

When Bill Sommers is confronted with a potential problem he has a series of mental maps to help him. He has discovered a number of response strategies that help in resolving problems quickly and without panic. The strategies are

1. *Consensus Building*—attempting to find common ground.

2. *Paraphrase*—A process of negotiating meaning with the speaker. Here you as the listener listen completely to the speaker and, at certain points, share what you understand you have heard with the speaker. In other words, you repeat back to the speaker *in your own words* what you feel you have heard. The speaker can tell you if you are correct or explain further if you are not. You must be careful not to "parrot phrase" by just repeating verbatim what you heard, because the speaker will think you did not really understand. Good paraphrasing demonstrates that the listener is sincerely attempting to understand what is being said.

3. *Silence, Empathy, and Accepting Nonjudgmentally*—You cannot listen if you are talking. Listening completely with empathy often defuses a situation. Responding with phrases like, "I understand how you must feel because I have felt that way before," go a long way to let the speaker know that you care. Accept what the speaker says without judgment during the input phase of the discussion. Do not argue at this time. Remember that perception is truth in the eye of the perceiver.

4. *Clarify and Probe for Specificity*—Develop skills as a questioner. Use neutral probing questions such as, "Help me understand

specifically what you feel the teacher did to your child." This is a place where Cognitive Coaching© training will help you.

5. *Chunking Up*—Sometimes the argument or discussion will be at a level where it is hard to find common ground. "Chunking up" means that you try to find a common ground above the fray. Sometimes I use the statement, "Both you and I want your daughter, Jane, to be successful in school and we are both looking for a way to make that happen."

6. *Third Position*—Finding an object that relates to the problem for both parties in conflict can often cool people down. While looking at a gradebook, a list of rules in a student handbook, or a chart on which you are diagramming, you are not glaring at each other eyeball to eyeball. Direct eye contact in a conflict can mean challenge and fight.

7. *The 3 Fs*—Felt, found, feel are three words you can use to form a statement that attends to empathy and understanding. It is a template to use while you are thinking of a next step. You say, "I *felt* that way before but I *found* out that I could . . . and now I *feel* that . . . " An example is, "I *felt* that special education students should be separated from mainstream students at one time. But I *found* out that both special education students and mainstream students benefit from working together and learning to deal with diversity. Now I *feel* that it is important to mainstream these students."

8. *"I Don't Know."*—How often I wished I had used this phrase before I found myself in real trouble. If you do not know, admit it. My favorite response at this time is, "I really don't know, but here is what I will do to find out . . . I will get back to you by . . . " If you say that, be sure that you do find out and get back.

Public schools are one of the few places where taxpayers can actually access the organization that spends their money. People need to feel heard and this process allows them to satisfy this need.

At this point, people will often feel embarrassed about how they appeared or they may still be posturing to save face. I like to make an ally if I can. I usually make this statement,

You know, Mr. Smith, your child is lucky to have you as a father. There are many parents today who would never come to see me about a problem. It is your job as a parent to do the best you can for your son. It is also my job to do the best I can for your son. When we work together we can make this school a better place for him. Please do not hesitate to come see me again if you have another problem.

As I have stated before, do not say this if you cannot mean it. Insincerity can cause you further problems.

There are those people whom you will never please. They are in your face to rub your nose in something and not to find solutions. My only recommendation is to be respectful and suggest that another meeting should be scheduled with your superintendent attending. Often these people will behave differently when more than one person representing the school is in the room. Above all, never give in to a bully.

MANAGING GROUP DYNAMICS

A friend of Bill's, Michael Grinder, said that, as an administrator, I must manage the group. I was shocked at his suggestion. I had spent most of my recent career trying to build constructive relationships that encouraged and sustained trust. My belief was that to have personal, reflective conversations with most people in my organization would lead to transformation of them and the organization. I had invested a lot of time in coaching skills to build one-to-one relationships. Most of my colleagues told me that fostering one-on-one interactions improved the school climate, and now he seemed to be telling me to manage top down.

Michael went on to tell me that what I was doing was great, but I still had to manage the group. I protested that he was wrong, stating that building relationships takes time but would, according to current research, work better in longer run.

He maintained his point of view and restated, "You have to manage one-to-one relationships *and* the group." I again said, "You just don't understand." He responded, "You must be able to manage the group to be a successful principal."

Because I trusted Michael, I began to rethink my position. Soon I discovered that he was right. I realized that I had to be able to manage individual relationships *and* be able to manage the group to be a successful principal.

Have you ever done your prework prior to meeting with a committee? You talked to everyone on the committee individually and felt that you had received agreement from all of the members on some point. Then, feeling smug, you walked into the meeting only to discover that everyone you had talked to seemed to have amnesia? This is where managing the group begins.

It seems as if whenever you pull together a group of bright people, a different dynamic affects the individuals. Even though individuals may have an opinion, when they are in a group a different relationship exists. Many individuals will not talk in a group about ideas they were willing to talk to you privately about. There are many reasons for this phenomenon, which include some members trying to dominate the conversation, some people not trusting the group well enough to risk a comment that may be criticized, some feeling their ideas will only waste the time of the group, and others being just too shy to speak up in an adult meeting. Principals must be able to work with groups, make decisions that will stick, and gain consensus in public as well as individually.

After considering Michael's challenge, I realized that it was up to me to work with individuals and manage the group. I finally realized that at times I, as principal, must stand up in front of the entire faculty and make a case for a vision, a decision, a new curriculum, or standards. At that time, I am not managing individuals with their individual talents, I am managing the group.

The point is that the principal must decide why the group is being convened, what he or she expects from the meeting, and then how he or she will lead the meeting. It is the same with the whole school. No matter how much shared decision making the staff and parents are involved with, the principal was hired to lead.

When managing the group, whether it is large or small, I may take the role of a highly credible person who is sending a clear message to the staff. I do this by making presentations, delivering information, using visuals, or using techniques like the "three chart method" (described earlier in this book). To do this I stand in front of the group, in a formal stance. I plan my approach carefully; it is often not a time for input.

On the other hand, sometimes I want group input and consensus. In that case, I present a more informal, relaxed posture. I may even sit down. My voice would invite participation; I would be approachable and welcome ideas from others. I would be seeking information. Instead of detailed charts, I would have outlines and blank chart paper with felt pens to record information. Ultimately, we would decide what to do by consensus.

In other words, there is a difference between managing a group and managing an individual. With the individual, you can work side by side, face to face, almost touching. A group, on the other hand, is more distant. Individuals can hide within while others dominate, so my techniques have to change to bring each individual into the group process.

It took time and effort to develop the skills of group management. I suggest a list of books (see the Resource section), and start practicing.

8

Assessing Students, Staff, and Schools

*If you don't know where you have been, how can you
tell where you are going? There is a difference between
feeling good and knowing you are good.*

When I started teaching, the word *assessment* meant grading. I
also remember at that time I became very concerned that too many
students were failing my classes. To overcome this problem, instead
of looking at my own teaching methods, I attempted to correct both
my students' and my own shortcomings by expanding the C bracket
on my grading scale. In other words, instead of a scale that went
from 100% to 90% = A, 89% to 80% = B, and 79% to 70% = C; my new
scale became 100% to 90% = A, 89% to 80% = B, and *79% to 65%* = C,
with a D being 64% to 55%.

Things went along fine with me using the system, and I gave
grading very little thought until one day when I was summoned to
testify in a court case involving one of my students. During the
cross-examination, I was asked about my grading scale. I responded
by describing the above scale. On hearing it, the judge, almost yelling at me, exclaimed, " You mean to tell me that a student could get a
passing grade in your class with only 55%! "

I was jolted into reviewing how my kids earn grades in my
classes. I decided that I was going about the process all wrong. I
came to the conclusion that to maintain my standards and be fair to
my students, I had to examine my program content and teaching
methods. At the same time, I went back to my older grading scale. In

125

other words, the problem was not the scale, it was me being too lenient. I was not modeling the concept of rising to standards and excellence

Not long after this, I was grading some pop quizzes that had a possibility of five points. As I corrected them, I included the points earned and a grade on the top of the page. For example, if a student had four correct out of five I wrote 4 and the letter B, and if a student had three correct out of five I wrote 3 and the letter C. A colleague walked by, and seeing what I was doing asked me if I graded on a percent system. I told him that I did and went on to explain my grading system. He then pointed out that if my C range was 70% to 79% and I was giving a student with three out of five points a letter grade of C, something was wrong. A three really represents 60%, which should be a D! He went on to point out that with a five-point quiz and no decimals there was no C range. In other words, a student could only earn an A, B, D, or F. Again, I was caught in an assessment trap. I had not truly thought out my grade point system.

Humbled, I realized that I did not understand grading. I had just been grading my students the way I was graded when I was in high school. It was obvious that there was more to it than met the eye. So I began investigating new ways to grade students and student work. It became the focus of my daily reading and I began to look for workshops about classroom grading.

ASSESSMENT VERSUS GRADING

As I progressed in my quest for a better grading system, I discovered that assessment was a much larger process, of which grading was only a small part. A grading system provides a student with a number or letter indicating the student's level of accomplishment, which is determined by some form of assessment.

Good assessment became my active pursuit. A complete coverage of the art of assessment is not possible in this book. There are many great books published that cover assessment very well from authors such as Grant Wiggins and Bena Kallick.

Classroom Assessment   Box 8.1

◆ Assessment should assess the students' progress as well as the teachers' effectiveness.

◆ A teacher should use multiple forms of assessment, including paper-and-pencil tests, portfolios (teacher and student), presentations, and projects.

◆ Students should always know what is expected of them and be provided with models of excellent work for comparison with their work.

◆ Teachers should provide instruction to students about how to self-assess.

◆ Parents should frequently be informed of students' progress or lack of it.

Over the years, I have developed strong feelings about grades and grading. At one time, I was ready to throw traditional grading out. I would still like to, but I do not think that is practical anymore. Too many schools, colleges, and parents expect grades. The University of California at Santa Cruz used to have a policy of no grades. Each student was provided with a narrative evaluation written by the professor. It was a noble idea, but it has been discontinued because students needed a grade average from the university when they applied to be accepted to a graduate school. Lazy professors also made a mockery of the process by using a multiple-choice program set up on the university computer to have computers write the evaluations from canned phrases.

Some of my feelings about grades are

Classroom Grades   Box 8.1

◆ Poor grades early in the semester should never carry so much weight that the student cannot dig himself or herself out of the hole. Students must have hope.

◆ Teachers must return work in a timely manner with comments that allow the students to learn from their mistakes.

◆ Students should never be kept in the dark about grades, including the grades that they are earning as well as the criteria used to develop the grades.

◆ Grades should never be arbitrary.

◆ Grades should not be based on first drafts and first attempts.

◆ Grades should be for students, not parents.

I discussed my feelings about grades during faculty meetings. We attempted to agree on when and how to use them. The purpose was to present a coherent grading system understood by parents and students. As a result, we had fewer problems with parents and a more consistent system.

Recently, I have developed a new idea about student grades. I feel that our grading system is all wrong. Most schools have a grading system that encourages cheating and does not encourage the pursuit of excellence. In most cases, it seems to me, the students who get As and Bs are the ones who have figured out the system. A person can kick back and do marginal work and still pass with a C. Would you like to have surgery from a doctor who only got a C in surgery? Of course not. So why do we allow students to get Cs for poor quality of work?

My daughter once complained that I got too upset over her earning a C in a subject. She asked, "What's wrong with Cs? They just say that you are average and what's wrong with average?" She was just getting dressed for school and was very particular about her clothes. I went to the dirty clothes hamper and chose an outfit for her. I handed it to her and said, "Here, wear these."

She said, "No! They are dirty."

I responded, "They are not very dirty. They are only average dirty."

I forget her response, but it made me think. Now I am convinced that we should never allow C work to be acceptable. I prefer a system where the grade you get is determined by the progress you are making toward excellence. An assignment should be reworked until it meets a standard for excellence that is appropriate for that student.

In other words, if a writing assignment is focused on the student writing complete sentences, then the teacher should not accept it until all the sentences in the essay are complete. The student should work and rework the essay until it meets the requirement. This is more like an apprenticeship system that strives for good craftsmanship. The number of completed assignments that meet the standards therefore could determine a grade. No accepted paper could be "average" because it would not be accepted until it was done correctly.

Another approach to grading is to have the students evaluate their own work with the guidance of the teacher according to a rubric and model work. Here the model work would allow students to see what was to be expected. Students would compare their work to the model according to specific steps outlined on a rubric. The grades would be determined by whether or not students made progress along the rubric, not just the quality of their work.

AUTHENTIC ASSESSMENT

The recent trend in assessment is often called *authentic assessment,* and there are many experts who have written volumes about how it should be done. We are strong proponents of assessment practices spelled out by Dr. Grant Wiggins and Dr. Bena Kallick. Basically the process is a triangulation approach to assessing student progress. Triangulation means that a student, teacher, or school is assessed using multiple methods that include paper-and-pencil standardized and criterion-referenced tests, student exhibitions and performances, and portfolios (see Figure 8.1).

TECHNOLOGY AND ASSESSMENT

Teachers and principals have been looking for ways to use personal computers for student assessment from the moment the computers arrived on the scene. In the beginning, they were not much more than a data bank used to store questions for tests and recording scores. I remember purchasing science test questions data banks for

Figure 8.1. Multiple Assessments

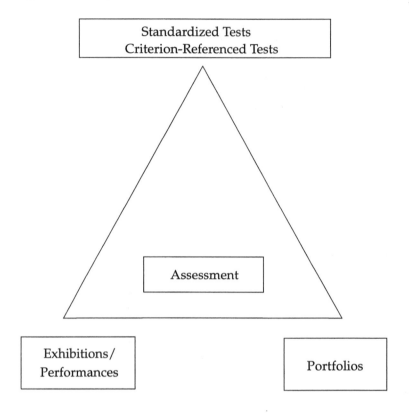

biology and earth science years ago. I used them to develop multiple-choice tests for grading my students. I have to admit that they were more a convenience than truly effective.

Today, there are some inexpensive commercial programs available to help teachers and administrators truly assess their students and programs. One such program is called TechPath© for Math, developed by Bena Kallick and the company Technology Pathways. This multifaceted program allows a mathematics teacher to select open-ended assessment questions from a list. Teachers are guided to an assessment question by making choices from a list of standards and strategies they would like to assess. The program is based on the National Council of Teachers of Mathematics standards.

After the students respond to the questions provided by the program, the teacher scores the papers in accordance with a rubric provided. The teacher is assisted by student examples called anchor papers supplied by the program. Finally, the teacher enters the student scores into a gradebook program rubric that rates students in a system that labels the work as Expert, Practitioner, Apprentice, or Novice in a series of categories that include understanding, strategies, and reasoning.

Teachers can use the program to print out statistics about each student and the entire class. They can use the results to group children in a number of ways according to their understanding of mathematics principles. In short, the program helps teachers to assess student understanding and progress. Using this information, teachers can self-assess and use the process to improve their teaching.

PORTFOLIOS

Portfolios are collections of carefully selected pieces of student or teacher work. Collections of work, along with comments made by the student or teacher explaining why each piece was chosen, can help to demonstrate student growth—or lack of it—over time in a particular area.

As an example, a student might begin a portfolio on writing. In this case, the student picks out examples of writing that represents his or her writing at that time. The student then compares these writings to examples of good writing and a rubric and then writes a brief statement about why these examples were chosen. The statement includes what needs to be done to improve the work to move it to another level on the rubric of good writing. The collection becomes a journey map of the progress that a student can review and use to demonstrate to another person or himself or herself growth over time in a particular skill.

The process seems simple and many teachers assume from a brief introduction that they know how to assist students in constructing portfolios. One of the problems administrators encountered in my district as teachers embraced the idea of portfolios was that they started to make random collections of work from students. Basically, this was nothing more than a scrapbook. This style of collection has little value to the teacher or the student. These collections become large and difficult to store. In most cases, all student work was stored in each portfolio without comment, defeating the purpose of portfolio assessment. Done correctly, the process of portfolio assessment is extremely complex. We feel that teachers who wish to use it should seek training by a competent staff developer.

Teachers and administrators can also benefit by constructing portfolios. Teacher portfolios should contain examples of whole lessons with student work included. Here again the teacher should include written explanations as to the reason for choosing each piece of work in the collection and project possible ways for improvement. Videotapes of the lesson can also be part of the portfolio.

Recent advances in computer storage devices allow for scanning material on a disk along with clips of the videotapes. Students can enjoy the production of this product and the portfolios for a class take up less space than paper portfolios.

As a principal in the Soquel School District, I was involved in the portfolio assessment project for administrators. Each administrator, from principal to superintendent, had to develop a portfolio demonstrating how his or her decisions and programs affected student learning.

As the year went on, each administrator, after consulting with the superintendent, began to collect evidence that supported the goals chosen at the start of the year. As each piece was selected, a note was attached explaining why it was chosen. At the end of the year, all the administrators made presentations of their portfolios to each other. It was not only good for each person to do, it was also fascinating for each of us to see what the other principals had been doing.

One year, I chose to demonstrate how students at my school benefited from my staff development programs. Throughout the year, I collected minutes from staff development planning meetings, my own journal entries, budget sheets demonstrating the money that was spent on staff development, and finally the observation forms that I filled out as I toured the campus and discovered that the teachers were using the training in their classrooms. I attached notes to each piece explaining why the piece was chosen. I did not statistically determine whether the program resulted in improved student learning, but I did clearly demonstrate that staff development was getting into the instructional program.

TEACHER EVALUATION

Perhaps the most difficult job most of us face is the regular, systematic evaluation of teachers. At the beginning of every year, I would promise myself that I would do a better job this year. I would do better at getting into the teachers' rooms more often while they are teaching during the year. I do not feel that it is right or effective to evaluate anyone with only one or two observations. It is also very embarrassing to meet with a teacher at the end of the year for evaluation and discover you only have one or two observations because you were too busy.

As a result of this concern, I developed a process that worked well for me. At the beginning of the year, usually before the teachers returned to school in the fall, I would send a letter reminding those on evaluation cycle that they would be asked for three goals at the beginning of the year. The goals were

1. A classroom goal designed to improve the educational quality of their program for each student
2. A professional development goal for themselves
3. A personal goal

Next, I took out my Daytimer and blocked out the year for teacher observations. It is important to write such days in the calendar so that you do not get too many days scheduled for other things. When you are sitting in a meeting between two other people and you are all consulting calendars looking for a common free day to meet, it is helpful to have blocked in the visitation days in your calendar. The people on each side of you cannot look at your calendar and assume that you are free when you are not. If you think that you can "make time later" for your evaluations, you are sadly mistaken. I have tried and failed and ended up at the end of the year embarrassed because I did not have sufficient observations to evaluate my teachers effectively.

Next, I make up a list of the teachers I will evaluate with columns. In the columns, I will eventually write in the dates of visitations. This page fits in my Daytimer (see Table 8.1). I can scan that page and determine immediately who has been visited and when and who needs a visit. I make sure that I visit teachers on evaluation

TABLE 8.1 Evaluation Schedule

Teacher	Visit #1	Visit #2	Visit #3	Visit #4	Visit #5
Adams	10/12	12/3			
Bronson	9/22				
Davis	9/22	12/3	2/9		
Ellison	10/1	11/15	2/9		
Franklyn	10/6				
Fundt	9/15	10/1	11/15	1/12	
Getty	10/12	11/15			

cycle with unscheduled drop-ins as often as I can as well as two preannounced visits. At the same time, I make a separate sheet for each teacher to fit in the Daytimer. I carry the Daytimer with me all the time so when I drop in on a teacher I first record the day and time on the column page and then take a few notes on the teacher's full page. At the end of the year, I have all the information that I need to write complete evaluations.

Two preannounced visits are scheduled with the teacher at the beginning of the year. Each evaluation takes three periods. The first, called the planning conference, and the third, called the reflecting conference, take place in my office during the teacher's preparation period. The second is a visit to the teacher's classroom while he or she is teaching to observe the lesson discussed in the planning conference (see the section on Cognitive Coaching© in Chapter 6). I feel that this process far exceeds the process of clinical supervision.

Finally, at the end of the year, I meet with each teacher for about an hour while we go over the evaluation report. Each report takes about 1 hour to prepare. With about 15 teachers to evaluate every year, it is easy to see why it is important to schedule the process from the beginning.

In summary, even though you say no, reprimand, evaluate, or deal with angry people remember to be

◆ Direct
◆ Respectful

◆ Reliable

◆ Consistent

◆ Attentive

◆ Clear

Evaluation is a tense time for a teacher. It is important that the principal be prepared with accurate visitation notes and notes on the results of the planning and reflecting conferences. This way the teacher is clearly made aware of why the contents of the evaluation have been written the way they are. Accurate data on the principal's part will help to avoid a confrontation.

With these qualities, you will maintain trust and respect from most of your colleagues and other people as you do a difficult part of your job from day to day.

WHOLE SCHOOL ASSESSMENT

I remember as a new principal making jokes about the state's standardized tests. As each report arrived, showing how poorly our students seemed to be doing, we would joke about how the assistant superintendent would do his "dance" in front of the board and make everything appear "all right." We played down our performance on the state standardized tests, and it was not long before our staffs picked up our attitude and also ignored the results. What we did not realize was that we were hurting ourselves in the long run.

We felt that state tests were of little value because the results arrived too late—often fall testing results would not arrive until July—and our curriculum was not aligned with the test. When the results arrived, I placed them in the teachers' room so that when they returned in the fall the results were there for them to examine.

If a school is to improve, it needs data about how its children are doing in relation to similar groups of students in other districts. We knew that but we did not think the state test was providing the data we needed. I know now that a school can gain knowledge from almost every form of assessment.

The process of growth is demonstrated with the spiral feedback diagram (Figure 8.2). I referred to this process in the first chapter. The principal and staff set goals and purposes and then plan to meet

Figure 8.2. Continuous Growth Through Feedback Spirals

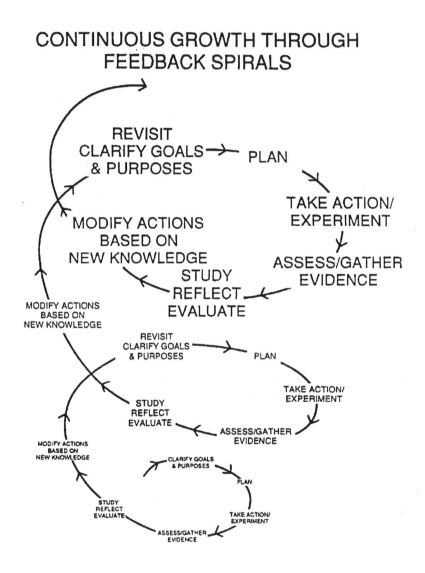

CONTINUOUS GROWTH THROUGH
FEEDBACK SPIRALS

SOURCE: Costa, A. L., & Kallick, B. (1995). *Assessment in the Learning Organization: Shifting the Paradigm* (p. 27). Alexandria, VA: ASCD. © 1995, ASCD. Reprinted by permission. All rights reserved.

those goals and purposes. Plans for assessing progress toward the goals should be set as part of the goal plan.

The next step is the implementation of the plan; assessment; and then, using the data, revisiting the plan. The assessment process should be multifaceted, employing more than just the state testing results.

In California, my middle school had a self-assessment process called Program Quality Review. It was a formal procedure that was established by the state and involved the staff and community. After we wrote an assessment report based on the self-study that followed state guidelines, a team from other schools visited our campus. They compared what they saw with the report to confirm the validity of the study. The very act of self-scrutiny helped us improve the quality of our school. Recently, the state changed the process and outside teams no longer are required to visit the schools. I firmly believe that this was a mistake. Now a school can write what it wishes without any outside confirmation.

9

Get a Life!

Remember that boss spelled backward is "double SOB!" With job demands and family responsibilities increasing, it is easy to see how a person can become cranky and turn into the "boss spelled backward." The question becomes, "How do administrators keep balance in their lives?" In this chapter, we discuss ways that many administrators have found to keep their sanity in the face of overwhelming odds.

THE 1-HOUR SABBATICAL

One morning, I kept track of the number of decisions I was asked to make from 7 AM to 8 AM, when the first period started. It came out to be 72! More than one a minute! The issues ranged from students asking directions to teachers requesting special permission to leave a few minutes early to make a medical appointment or to miss a meeting to questions from parents. Secretaries also needed information, signatures, and help with student problems during that time. It is no doubt that school administrators have very busy days. Their time feels as if it is not their own and everyone wants a piece of them.

If I want to get something done early in the morning, I have to sneak in and leave the lights off in the office. As soon as people know that I am on campus, they always want something. Yet we all know that we need time to ourselves just to keep our sanity. I learned of a technique that worked for me that I call the "1-hour sabbatical."

When the day's pressures built up too high and I felt that I needed a time out, I would tell my secretary and vice principal that I would be gone for about 1 hour. I did not tell them where I would be or how to get hold of me. Then I either went for a walk or to a coffee shop, where I sat in a quiet corner with a cup of coffee and the newspaper, a book, or my journal. I was never far from the campus and I did have a cell phone that my personal secretary knew the phone number of, but she was sworn to not call or give out the number unless it was absolutely necessary. After about an hour, I would head back to the office refreshed and ready to go again. This worked wonders to restore my mental and emotional balance.

JOURNALING

Somewhere I heard the statement, "Writing is nature's way of showing us just how screwed up our thinking is!" In my case it is very true. When I have to think clearly, propose a solution or idea during a meeting, or plan, I need to write it down.

The discovery of journal writing (also described earlier) was a great release for me as a teacher and an administrator. It was Art Costa who first introduced me to the kind of journal I am referring to. This journal is not used as a daily diary; rather it is used for reflections from time to time on a "semiregular" basis. I carry one everywhere with me and, depending on the day, use it several times a day or sometimes only once or twice a week. My journal consists of a small 8 1/2-by-5 1/2-inch (half of a regular page) loose leaf or spiral-bound book. Recently, I have started making my own, using a plastic spiral binding. Lightweight and extremely portable, it is easy to carry and it is almost always with me.

I prefer to write in my journal with a fountain pen because it feels good and forces me to slow down my thinking. Some people like to journal on a computer, but I find that a hand-written journal is more kinesthetic, thoughtful, easy to carry, and not dependent on any outside power. I can write almost anywhere. I carry mine with me almost everywhere I go and write in it when I have time and the spirit moves me. I would be lost without it.

We feel that writing in a journal is so useful that both Bill and I gave journals to each member of our staffs. Each teacher received the journal along with an outline for using it. There were several rules:

Absolute Journal Rules

1. You will *never* be forced to share your journal with anyone.

2. You will *never be asked to turn* your journal in.

3. You *must bring your journal* to every teachers' meeting and staff development training.

4. The journal is yours to keep and to use whenever you wish. When it is full, ask for another.

How to Use Your Journal

1. There are no rules about what to do in your journal. You may write, draw, list, and who knows what else as you wish.

2. Some good starter ideas are

   I am wondering about . . .
   Something that puzzles me is . . .
   I am bothered about . . .
   Today was the . . .

3. Your journal is a place for reflection, ideas, concerns, thinking, and other ideas limited only by your imagination.

At each faculty meeting, there was always time to use our journals. Usually this was when we were getting ready to make a major decision or have a deep discussion about something. Whenever we do this, our discussions were deeper, more complete, and had more people involved and we made better decisions.

REFLECTIVE PRACTICE AND JOURNALS

At South High in Minneapolis, Bill Sommers started a reflective practice program. The staff agreed to meet once a month for 2 hours after school off-site. They chose to use a community facility that overlooked a lake, making it a pleasant place to relax and reflect. They also decided to meet once a week in dyads or triads for a minimum of 1 hour. Finally, they decided to journal each day. Journaling was probably the most difficult to incorporate into the program. About 50% of the people did start journaling. Teachers could choose anything to reflect about through writing, but they were encouraged to reflect about education. Most of them preferred to write about what they were doing or planning for their classrooms.

The reflective practice group became a leadership force in his building and a catalyst for staff development. The group also provided an avenue to coordinate with district agendas and develop site-based goals.

Because the group members were responsible for planning their own personal and professional growth, they created an environment where their own as well as group goals could be achieved. This also took the weight off the site administrator as the person solely promoting and planning staff development. I would certainly call this empowerment!

DEVELOPING A PERSONAL SUPPORT SYSTEM

My first job as principal was of a small continuation high school in California. White Oak High School was in a district I had taught in for over 20 years and all the teachers were friends as well as colleagues. I was expecting to be accepted as a friend and colleague as I walked in the door of White Oak. I was shocked when I realized that I was treated in a friendly way, but not as a true friend. I had crossed the line to administration and was no longer looked on in the same trusting way. I was the new and suspicious boss.

The lesson I learned was that once you become a principal you are often alone on the campus because of your position. Your life has changed as far as personal, collegial relationships are concerned. You can no longer trust your colleagues to keep private conversations confidential. Your one partner, your personal secretary, is the one person who is always there, but even though he or she works only for you, you must guard what you say at first. In most cases, your secretary is not a confidential employee and may not be a person in whom you can truly confide. So how do you go about developing a supportive system for yourself?

Even at larger schools where you have a vice principal or two or three, remember that they are still your employees and cannot be truly relied on to be part of your support system without a careful development process to build trust. Since you are alone at the top at your site, you must develop a support system on which you can rely. This is a person or persons to whom you can go to unload problems, think out loud with, confide in, and to ask advice. Such persons must keep your confidences and understand the problems of your office and be empathetic. Believe me, you will need this network, which takes time to build but is indispensable.

As a middle school principal, I was able to develop a support system that included my wife, a close friend and principal from another district, two principals in my district, my vice principal, my secretary, and a teacher at my school. These people I could rely on for different situations. My support system developed slowly, over time. Of course, my wife had been my adviser and confidante for a long period of time. The others became trusted friends with shared educational experience. The process begins with small confidences you share with a person. It does not take long before you know whether or not the person you shared something with had kept it confidential. It really takes an intuitive feeling, but over time you discover whom you can trust and whom you cannot.

Requirements for a Support Person or System

◆ The people must be confidentially reliable. When asked, they do not tell anybody.

◆ They must be readily accessible—easy to get to and willing to listen.

◆ They must have the time.

◆ Depending on the situation you need to discuss, they must understand your situation and, if at all possible, have been in a similar situation.

◆ Each person must be willing to be your support person. I always asked if it was OK for them to help me with each situation that I brought up. I was always respectful of their time and never just assumed that they wanted to listen to me. I usually approached them with a statement like, "I am having a problem with a teacher. I need to talk to someone about it. Do you have the time?"

The following people are examples of my regular support system:

My Wife—A person who had been a teacher and has a great mind about education, she never failed to speak her mind and was always an interested and trusted critic.

Personal Friend/Principal—This man was my most confidential support person. We had a longtime relationship and knew that whatever we said in confidence would be kept confidential. He was also a person with experience and could be relied on to give good advice and listen thoroughly. I could disagree with him philosophically without either of us becoming upset.

Two Principals From My District—One was at a school that shared the same building with my school and the other was an extremely experienced administrator with the habit of "telling it like it is." These relationships took an effort to build and developed over time.

The Vice Principal at My School—He had been at the school for some time and was a fantastic partner with all the history of the school and community. He helped me anticipate the problems I could run into. He was always open to brainstorm possibilities and then was very imaginative at follow-through once we had determined our direction. Another plus was that he and I saw eye to eye on most things.

My Secretary—She was one of the most loyal people I have ever known. I never discovered a situation where she was not confidential. I often remarked that no interrogator using any method could break her. She was always open to creative suggestions and kept me informed about what was going on in the office. I could ask her advice about anything without fear of it becoming general knowledge.

A Teacher—Most administrators find it ill advised to use a teacher as a confidant, but one teacher was invaluable to me. Early in my career as a principal, I found the need to become a better writer. Past memos often annoyed me, as did other documents issued by my principals, because they could not write well and did not seem to want to learn to write well. Their writings were often confusing, leading to misunderstanding by the people they were meant for. I asked this English teacher to help me become a better writer. She agreed, and in the course of her reviewing my writing, I had to trust her. I never had a reason to think that she talked about personal things or decisions that I was considering with the staff. I trusted her and she trusted me. It was a leap of faith based on good personal intuition, which is a skill I developed over time.

CLARIFYING YOUR OWN PERSONAL
AND EDUCATIONAL VALUES AND BELIEF SYSTEM

I once read that Robert Fulghum, author of *All I Really Need to Know I Learned in Kindergarten* (1993), wrote his best-selling poem as a result of attempting to set down his credo about life. He explained that over several years he annually wrote out his beliefs and values. At first, the document was very long, and each year he attempted to make it more concise and to the point. The result is familiar to all of us.

After reading about Robert Fulgum and his credo, I decided that it would be very good for me to do the same about education. I struggled over the first edition and then, after bouncing it off my support system, decided to give it to my staff. One of my support people told me that I should be careful, because if I gave it to the staff they would hold me to it. I said that I hoped that they would, because if I could not defend my beliefs and values I should reexamine them.

After a year, I reworked the document and although it is not as elegant as Fulgum's, I include the second version here. The experience was well worth the effort. I deliberately began the title with "Rough Draft . . . " because I intend to constantly evaluate the statement in light of new learning.

Rough Draft—Rough Draft—Rough Draft—Life Is a Rough Draft

Thoughts on a Personal Philosophy of Education
by Dave Schumaker

The following represents my personal educational philosophy. It is not meant to be a definitive end to my thinking about education and the responsibilities of students and teachers. I wrote my first draft in the fall of 1988. A couple of years later, I decided to revisit my original attempt to write my philosophy, but first I wrote some ideas down in my journal and then pulled out my original attempt and compared the two. It was interesting what was new and what was intentionally or accidentally left out of the old statement. I still feel that if I ever get set in my ways and quit changing—quit growing—I should hang it up and do something less significant such as painting by numbers or doing dot-to-dot puzzles.

Education is for the students. All of an educator's energy needs to go to keeping the student's needs in mind. Students must focus on themselves and the task at hand. That task is learning from a variety of situations and teaching each other and the others around us. Students' self-esteem comes from knowing the hows and whys of life and feeling able to accomplish things. They must have choices and feel free to choose their path with knowledge and confidence as they progress through life.

Students, to have the greatest chance of success, must

- Know why they are asked to do things by teachers
- Regularly self-assess and keep track of their progress
- See and recognize evidence of their own growth
- Recognize that just about everything is connected to everything else in some way
- Persist when faced with a struggle or a tough situation
- Not be satisfied with less than the best—have high expectations for themselves
- Know the goals of their own education
- Work with others
- Like themselves
- Have a joy for learning
- Be amused by life

The goals of education for students should be to

- Learn to read for comprehension, joy, and information
- Learn to communicate through writing, speaking, and art
- Learn to understand and use basic math
- Learn to solve problems using a variety of problem-solving strategies
- Learn what to do when they do not know what to do
- Learn to have empathy for others

- ◆ Learn to have empathy for the earth and all of its systems
- ◆ Learn deeply
- ◆ Become a responsible citizen
- ◆ Know who they are and understand their history
- ◆ Learn for intrinsic reasons
- ◆ Develop a strong sense of their own values
- ◆ Be able to use technology for a better life but not be so involved with it that they drop out of society and limit social interaction

For students to accomplish these goals, teachers must provide them with

- ◆ "Real-world problems" to learn with
- ◆ Choices and variety
- ◆ Opportunities to learn emphasizing various modalities and intelligences
- ◆ Opportunities to self-evaluate
- ◆ A risk-free learning environment
- ◆ A stimulating program in a calm learning environment
- ◆ Instruction in the use of technology
- ◆ Skills to enable them to access information and enhance thinking and problem solving
- ◆ Reasons why they are being asked to do something
- ◆ A consistent set of behavior expectations
- ◆ Developmentally appropriate tasks
- ◆ Love

On Being a Teacher

Since, in reality, "nothing can be taught, only the means of learning can be provided," according to Louis Alberto Machado (1980, p. 15), teachers have their work cut out for them. They have charges that are with them all day long, in a captive mode, completely at the whim of what they would have them do. They must understand that it has been shown that the time of day a student spends in class is, in the child's mind, the most unproductive time of the day. Much of this is due to the kind of work that teachers provide for the students to do. It makes teaching one of the most stressful and difficult of all jobs, and if it is done correctly it can often lead to burn out from too much effort.

Teachers talk about themselves as professionals, but often act like blue-collar workers. Many complain about time out of their classrooms for their own learning and grumble when asked to spend time on staff development projects. Although some exceptions to the rule are "We work too hard to have to learn more and, besides, I know all I need to know about teaching—leave me alone and let me 'teach.'"

Teachers will become true professionals when they

◆ Know how and why they ask children to do something
◆ Become as interested in keeping up with research in their profession as doctors, scientists, and mechanics
◆ Know how the mind develops and works
◆ Continuously self-evaluate
◆ Form collegial relationships
◆ Question what they do
◆ Coach and get coached
◆ Realize that all children can learn
◆ Hold high expectations for all children
◆ Take an active part in the decisions that affect them

It has been over 3 years since I wrote my first philosophy. I do not want anyone to think that I feel that I have achieved all that I have stated here as an educator; on the contrary, these are aspirations of what I feel I, and all teachers for that matter, should strive for in our careers.

Abraham Maslow (1998) said,

Growth takes place when the next step forward is subjectively more delightful, more joyous, more intrinsically satisfying than the previous gratification with which we have become familiar and even bored; that the only way we can ever know that it is right for us is that it feels better subjectively than any alternative. The new experience validates itself rather than by any outside criterion. (p. 197)

At the beginning of this and the original paper, I stated, "Life is a rough draft." I truly feel that way, and this document represents what I feel about education at this moment. I have changed over the years. I did not begin with most of these ideas, nor have they remained the same since I first wrote about them; rather, they have grown in me over time, and I am sure that they will continue to grow in the future. For that matter, if you should discover that I have ceased to grow, please escort me out of the building and tell me my time in education is up. It will be time to do something less significant, such as politics or medicine.

KEEPING YOUR PERSONAL IDENTIFICATION— THE DIFFERENCE BETWEEN YOU AND YOUR POSITION

I vividly remember the feeling that day when I was caught in the vise of reality. I had had a problem with my vice principal. I did not agree with something that he was doing and I needed to tell him. I knew he was not going to be happy about my action. It especially bothered me because he was my closest confidant on the campus and part of my support system. It was early in my first year as principal of the middle school and I was struggling with the fact that I often had to tell adults what to do when I felt that they should have known for themselves. I felt that I was becoming unpopular and even hated by some!

The feeling haunted me and I decided to do something about it. I met with a counselor friend of mine for two sessions. He asked me to write about my feelings in my journal and we talked about my writings. Very quickly, he guided me to my own decision. I realized that on the job I was the principal. When I was making decisions and relaying my decisions to those who were involved, these actions came from the principal, not Dave. If the interaction was unpopular, it was the principal who took the blame. The person, Dave, was somewhat above the fray. If I remained professional, it was Dave the principal who they were mad at, not Dave the person.

From that point on, I never had a major problem conveying anything to anyone working for me. This process allowed me to see that there was a difference between the person and the position of boss.

At school everything I did was tainted by the fact of my position. I was always shocked to find people rushing to do something just because I was caught brainstorming or thinking out loud about possibilities. I had to be very clear about my intentions. If I was talking, I clarified by saying, "I'm brainstorming now, so please don't jump to the conclusion that I want you to act at this moment."

I also had to constantly make sure that I took care of the person within. This meant that I attempted to go home at 5:00 PM every day that I did not have later responsibilities, such as a school board meeting or a game to supervise, and to keep the weekend for myself. For a principal, it is easy to be eaten up by the job. It is a given that no matter how much time you spend, you can always spend more at your job. I know principals who have ruined marriages because they worked at their job too long and had nothing left for the family or themselves.

This need to keep something for my family and myself was highlighted by an incident. I was leaving for work after a summer vacation. It was my first day back on the job and the start of a new school year. As I was going out the door, my wife stopped me and said, "This year I had better be someone other than someone penciled in on your calendar!" I was jolted into the reality that she had let me get my feet on the ground with this job for a year and now wanted some of my time that she could depend on. It caused me to change my attitude toward my job and my personal responsibilities.

At the end of my first year as principal, I developed high blood pressure and was taking daily medication. During one of the moments when I was feeling particularly jittery, my superintendent, Richard Patterson, stopped by and noticed that I was not my usual self. He told me to take a day off and not to check in during that day. He highlighted the fact that I could not do my job well if it made me sick or forced me to quit. I realized that I needed to develop some ground rules to survive the job and feel that I was doing a good job as principal at the same time.

Howard McCluskey has a theory about adult learning. It is called the *theory of margin* (Merriam, 1993). People do not have perfect control over their lives. In schools you must always be prepared for the unexpected and to live with ambiguity. McCluskey's margin is the ratio of the relationship between "load," the personal and social demands required to do the job with a minimum level of autonomy, and "power," the ability to make things happen on the job (see Figure 9.1).

Figure 9.1. Load–Power

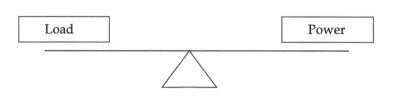

Load is broken down into two parts, external and internal. The external load consists of tasks involved in normal life requirements (family, work, and community responsibilities), and the internal load consists of life expectancies developed by people (aspirations, desires, and future expectations). Power is a combination of external resources, such as family, social, and financial resources, as well as internal resources, accumulated skills and experience.

Balancing the demands of load and power takes time and energy. Principals need to help themselves and their staff members discover resources to deal with the increasing loads. It is crucial to develop a surplus of power by increasing resources if one is to survive the intensity of today's public schools.

WHAT ROLES DO YOU PLAY?

Take this survey. Rank the order of the roles that you play from the one you spend the most time with to the one you spend the least time with.

_____ 1. Mother or father

_____ 2. Sister or brother

_____ 3. Spouse

_____ 4. Principal

_____ 5. Grandparent

_____ 6. Son or daughter

_____ 7. Colleague

_____ 8. Friend

_____ 9. Coach or adviser

_____ 10. Consultant

_____ 11. _____

Are you paying attention to what is important to you? Is your life a balance or a ballast to you? Remember, no one on his or her deathbed ever said, "I wish I had spent more time at work." What attributes are most important for you to have that provide resources to people when you are in the roles you have ranked? What are you doing to apply these attributes to your job?

PERSONAL WORK QUESTIONNAIRE— HOW ARE YOU DEVELOPING YOUR RESOURCES?

Take some time to think about yourself further. Use your journal to record your thoughts about the following questions.

1. What physical exercise do you do on a regular basis? How often?

2. What are the three most important issues your school or district is facing right now?

3. How do you think your organization should respond to each one?

4. What are two or three major projects you are working on at the present time?

5. What are boosters for your position? What are barriers to your position?

6. What books have you read in the past year? What did you learn?

7. What workshops have you attended? What did you learn?

8. What are the major accomplishments you have made in your job at the present time?

9. What are the major issues you still must complete?

10. What are five positive characteristics that describe you? Give examples for each.

Now read back over your reflections. Are you satisfied? What would you like to change? When and how will you make those changes? Make a contract with yourself to readjust your priorities and start to make those changes. Set achievable short-term and long-term goals for yourself. Write two letters to yourself about what you are attempting to do. Include your goals. Place them in separate self-addressed envelopes and number the envelopes 1 and 2. Now give them to a friend or secretary with the instructions to mail the first one to you after 2 weeks, and the second after 2 months. As you receive each letter, take time to revisit your journal, assess your progress, and then recommit yourself to yourself.

SELF-RENEWAL

When principals become completely wrapped up in their job, it is easy for them to be so involved with the daily problems and concerns for their staff that they neglect their own professional development. New research on education and learning is coming out every day, and it is very difficult to keep up. As part of taking care of themselves, today's principals must plan for their own professional development. Without this emphasis, they will soon fall behind and not be as effective as educational leaders.

The public is constantly raising the expectations it holds for school principals. To do a good job for children, principals must take care of themselves personally and professionally. Without this self-care, today's principals will burn out quickly and soon become ineffective. Keep in mind that our job is to create the best educational environment for each child in our schools. We can only do that if we are mentally and physically healthy and if we remain intellectually at the top of our profession.

10

The Principal's Toolbox

Anecdotes and Hints
for Survival in a Cruel, Cruel World

It was 9:00 AM and I was sitting in my office in an emergency meeting with a seventh-grade girl, a police detective, a representative of the Child Protective Services, and the school counselor. It all started at 7:30 that morning when we received a tip from a neighbor that the girl's father had been sexually molesting her for several years. We had immediately informed the authorities, who responded immediately. The meeting was somber. The girl was sobbing out the details of a serious crime and I was sitting there dressed up as a frog.

Yes, a frog. It was my first Halloween as principal of the middle school and I had donned a bright green frog outfit, complete with webbed fingers and webbed feet, at home that morning before I drove to work. I did not bring a change of clothes. Why did someone not tell me? Why did I not think it out?

I always seemed to have clothing problems. Earlier that year, I went on an overnight trip to Ontario, California. I decided to travel light, with only a change of underwear and a spare shirt. On arriving at the hotel late in the evening, I ordered dinner and the waitress spilled the plate of spaghetti in my lap. I made my presentation the following morning with an ugly red stain on the front of my pants.

The lesson for all of us is *always* have a change of clothes nearby. During your tenure as a principal, there will be a time when you need to look professional. Keep an emergency outfit at school and always travel with a spare pair of pants.

Most of us have had to learn many lessons the hard way. Invention usually happens on the spot out of necessity. Bill and I have assembled a tool kit of odds and ends, inventions and hints that have helped smooth the way we work.

SUBSTITUTE TEACHERS

The principal has to deal with many difficult problems daily. Working with substitutes is high on the problem list. We either do not have them when we need them or students do not take them seriously when they are there. Even teachers do not trust them to really teach and provide them with "substitute"-proof lessons (usually a videotape or a series of black line dittos to dull their minds). Most students and teachers do not consider substitute days teaching days.

At New Brighton Middle School, I came up with a system that made our school the most desirable school for subs to work at and literally guaranteed that we got the "cream of the crop" of the substitute list. It also helped to make substitute days teaching days. To start with, I personally met with every new substitute in the morning of the first day he or she came to work at my school. The substitute calling service was told to tell the substitute to arrive on campus one-half hour earlier than usual to meet with me. This was intended to be a welcoming and orienting meeting to explain our procedures. It was also to inform them of our intent to be an effective substitute support system to make them truly a part of our teaching staff. During that meeting, I gave them a triple-page carbonless form with the following statement at the top:

> We consider you part of our staff while you are working at New Brighton. During your work here we expect you to respect our students, enforce all the rules, follow the teacher's lesson plan, and fill out this form, leaving a copy in the teacher's mailbox and a copy with the principal's secretary. Failure to fill out this form completely and return it will result in your name being removed from our substitute list. You will not work here again.
>
> You are a professional and we expect you to ask for help if you need it. Our students are expected to treat all teachers,

substitutes included, and other students with respect at all times. We expect you to help us enforce that concept. Failure to ask for help for any reason is considered a weakness. We expect to support you as if you were a permanent teacher on the staff. We want you and your students to benefit from your being here.

The form went on to ask questions about the teacher's lesson plans and about each class taught, with a checklist of tasks to complete at the end of the day, including instructions on how to shut the windows and lock the door.

Each substitute also received a copy of the student handbook, an abbreviated copy of the teacher handbook, a classroom schedule, and a bell schedule. At that first meeting, I also personally handed the substitute the teacher's lesson plan for the day with an up-to-date seating chart.

Each teacher had on file in the office an emergency lesson plan. This plan was to be used in the event that something happened and the teacher could not prepare a current plan.

Good substitutes were considered treasures. We protected them and made them feel very welcome. The vice principal and I constantly checked on them throughout the day and immediately followed up if they needed help. Students knew that if they caused problems for a substitute they would be held responsible by the administration and their teacher. If a substitute left a negative comment about a class, I checked to see what the teacher was doing to correct the situation. As a result, we always had substitutes when we needed them and we heard again and again that New Brighton was the best place to work as a substitute teacher.

VIDEO CAMERAS—THE EXTRA SUPERVISOR ON CAMPUS

One year we had a drinking fountain vandal. During lunch someone was removing parts of a drinking fountain in a remote area of the campus that was difficult to supervise. It seemed as if every time we fixed the fountain it would be vandalized within a day.

To solve the problem, I set up a video camera on a tripod in a classroom across from the drinking fountain. During lunch on the second day, the fountain was vandalized again. It was easy: We rewound the tape and played it and there was our vandal. The picture showed him walking up, looking around, taking pliers out of his pocket, and dismantling the fountain. The video made it hard for the parents to deny that their child was guilty.

From that day on, we used the camera whenever we felt the need for another set of eyes. It is easy to have it sitting inside a room focused out a window recording for up to an hour.

DISCIPLINE

Discipline Records

Keeping track of discipline on a campus can be time consuming. The system described here is the most efficient I have ever used.

Each teacher had a stack of carbonless copy forms for referral of discipline problems. The discipline rule was

1. The teacher dealt with the first two discipline problems with a student unless the violation was serious, such as fighting, carrying weapons, or verbally assaulting the teacher.

2. Each time there was a problem, the teacher filled out the form describing the incident and the punishment. Especially, the teacher had to show that the parent was contacted both times.

3. One copy of the form was given to the student, one to the student's advisory teacher, one kept by the teacher, and one was filed in the staff room.

4. On the third offense, the teacher gave all the forms to the vice principal.

At this point, the vice principal would go to the staff room and take out the student's discipline file. The filing cabinet for discipline forms was located in the staff room. It had one drawer for each grade level. In each drawer were file folders, one for each student who had received a referral, and some blank folders. After writing a referral, the file copy was filed by the teacher. All the teacher had to do was open the drawer and find the student's name and drop in the referral copy. If there was no file folder for the student, it meant that that particular student had not been in trouble yet, so the teacher took a blank folder and wrote the student's name on the tab and then filed the form.

The vice principal took the student's file out and consulted it before calling in the student for the next step in discipline. In the file would be copies of the first two referrals from the teacher along with any others from other teachers or other years. This allowed him to see if the problem was with just one teacher or more. It also allowed him to check to see that the teacher had made the original two contacts with the parent. If not, the vice principal returned the student referral to the teacher. Punishment varied from flag list (see below) all the way to suspension or expulsion.

At the end of the year, a secretary discarded all the folders from the outgoing class and prepared for the new students coming in the fall. Sixth-grade folders went down to the seventh-grade drawer, seventh down to the eighth, and the top drawer stood ready and waiting for the incoming sixth-grade class.

Flag List

When students' infractions were not major, they would be assigned hours on the flag list. Students had the choice of detention after school or working off the hours helping on the campus. There were jobs to choose from, working for teachers, custodians, or the vice principal doing campus cleanup. Once a student was assigned hours on the flag list he or she could not attend any school functions, participate in sports, or receive a yearbook until the hours were worked off. We even had an agreement with another middle school in our area that if students transferred they would still owe the hours.

DAYTIMER

How often do you find that at the end of the day you have notes written on everything from Post-its to napkins reminding you of this or that? Or you were certain that you would remember things you were told as the day went on, but at the end, when you tried to remember them all, you could not. Some things just fell by the wayside.

I decided to consolidate all of my notes and records in my Day-timer so that everything would be in one place. I set up the 5 1/2-by-8 1/2-inch notebook with a series of tabbed sections:

- School schedule—bell times, teachers' room numbers, class schedule
- Monthly calendar
- Meetings—a page for each regular meeting: school board, Home and School Club, site council, teachers, department heads, administrators, superintendent
- To do list
- Phone numbers
- Evaluation—an overall schedule for teacher observations (see section on Teacher Evaluation in Chapter 8), a page for each teacher on cycle, and some observation forms

Each item was preceded by a dash "-." Once I had attended to the item I put a vertical line through the dash, making it a "+." This allowed me to quickly scan the list to see what had been addressed or not. As each of these pages was filled, I removed it and stored it in a file as a log of what had been done with each item. I took my Day-timer to all meetings and teacher visitations.

3-BY-5-INCH CARDS

Another great organizer I owe to a good friend of mine, Martin Krovetz from San Jose State University. It requires that you always carry some 3-by-5-inch cards in your pocket. Throughout the day as you encounter questions to answer or things to do, you write each one on a separate card. Then, from time to time during the day, you sort through the stack and prioritize the items by placing the most urgent cards on the top. As you deal with each problem, you aggressively tear up the card and throw it away, giving you a perverse sense of satisfaction at getting another thing off your back. At the end of the day, you sort what is left into three stacks. Stack 1 has items to be done *before* you leave for the day, Stack 2 contains items that must be dealt with the first thing in the morning of the next day, and Stack 3 contains items that can be put off for a time. I now carry a small leather wallet called a pocket secretary with 3-by-5-inch cards. One card fits in a frame on the front of the wallet and is ready to write on at all times. There are two pockets in it, one for extra cards and the other for business cards. It fits in a shirt pocket or the inside pocket of a jacket and travels with me all the time.

STAND-UP DESK

I have heard that visual people have messy desks because out of sight means out of mind. I always have a messy desk. Throughout the day, a principal is constantly receiving papers: mail, memos, notes, periodicals, advertisements, and so on. I used to sit by my desk and sort the material into piles: one for immediate action, one to file, one for action later, one to throw away, and one for those items I am not sure what to do with. Soon there were piles every-where. Then I hit on a great idea. I built a desk on top of a low book-case so that it was comfortable to work at while standing. On the left was an in-basket and on the right was a wastebasket. The desk sloped so that it was impossible to stack papers on it. My secretary put all of my incoming mail in the in-basket. Throughout the day, when time permitted, I would take papers from the in-basket and immediately deal with them. For instance, if one required a signa-ture I would sign it and put it in my secretary's in-basket. The next might be something I did not want, so I dropped it into the wastebas-ket. Maybe the next needed filing, so I filed it. I scanned periodicals and flagged pages to read and put them in my briefcase for later or read them on the spot. Basically, the arrangement forced me to han-dle the work efficiently. I still had trouble keeping my desk neat, though.

STAND-UP MEETING

Each morning, right after the first bell rang and classes had started, I returned to the office from campus supervision. As I entered and walked to my office, my secretary would grab her copy of my calendar and follow me. We would stand there in my office with the door closed for about 5 minutes to coordinate our calendars and plan the day. I kept the original calendar with me so that I could make my own decisions on how my time was scheduled. She would update her copy each day and confirm tentative appointments with me during the meeting or throughout the day. This way she was never surprised by my schedule and I was always up to date on what I needed to do.

I also discovered that when people drop in unannounced I could get up out of my chair and meet them standing as they entered. I would remain standing and would not ask them to sit unless I determined that they had a serious problem. By remaining standing, I encouraged the visitor to be quick and to the point. It prevents people from wasting your time and allows you to be cordial without inviting them for long visits.

EMERGENCY DRILL

With the increase of violence on school campuses, the job of principal not only becomes more complex, it also becomes downright dangerous. The possibility of shooters on campus is no longer a fictional horror story and the question therefore becomes, "How does the campus react during an attack?" I had a plan in place that was discussed thoroughly with the teachers and staff. The plan was as follows:

1. Anyone who saw a gun or a stranger on campus would immediately call the office from the closest phone. (Every room had a phone to the office.)

2. The office secretary who received the call would immediately notify the principal and vice principal by voice, phone, or radio and then call the police.

3. An administrator would authorize the campus warning. The warning was an announcement over the all-call stating, "This is an emergency drill. This is an emergency drill."

4. On hearing that announcement, teachers knew that they must keep the students in their room until an all-clear was announced. No attempt should be made to lock the doors, since that would require teachers to go outside the room to do so, making themselves vulnerable to attack.

5. Students in outdoor classes such as PE would lie down on the grass.

6. Only the police or the principal could call off the drill.

THE CUSTODIAN

I was told by a very wise adviser just before I took my first job as a teacher that the two most important people to have on your side in a school are the principal's secretary and the custodian. I can remember that it was easier to go directly to the custodian and ask favors than go through channels. It seemed that things got done more quickly for me that way.

One day, after my second year as principal, one of my custodians walked into my office and sat down and said, "I just can't keep up with all the teacher requests." I realized that I had not given much thought to how the custodians and maintenance people received work orders. There was a district form for large projects, but for all the little ones the process was informal, so that some custodians were being asked to do too much.

There were two major problems with the "system" that had been in place since before I came to the school:

1. Teachers often asked the wrong person to do a job. Custodians were being asked to do maintenance and vice versa.

2. Only friendly and congenial workers were being asked to do things for the teachers. The more prickly workers were avoided, so that some people were overloaded with requests.

I do not like complex paperwork, so I developed the form shown in Figure 10.1. Each teacher was told to stop personally asking workers to do a job. Workers were told to not accept verbal requests from teachers. Instead the teacher filled out the half-sheet form shown in the figure.

After filling out the form, the teacher gave the form to me. I would review each request to determine need and cost. If I approved it, I initialed the form and assigned it to a custodian or maintenance worker. I made a copy to retain and placed the original in the assigned worker's mailbox. When the job was completed, the

Figure 10.1. Work Request

```
┌─────────────────────────────────────────────────────────┐
│                                                           │
│   Date Requested _____Date_____        │
│   Completed_____                               │
│                                                           │
│   Requested by _____        │
│                                                           │
│   Location of Work Need _____        │
│                                                           │
│   Request:_____        │
│                                                           │
│          _____        │
│                                                           │
│          _____        │
│                                                           │
│          _____        │
│                                                           │
│          _____        │
│                                                           │
│          _____        │
│                                                           │
│                                                           │
│                                                           │
│   Assigned to_____Date_____        │
│                                                           │
│   Principal's Initials _____                 │
│                                                           │
└─────────────────────────────────────────────────────────┘
```

worker wrote the date completed on the top and returned it to me. This not only allowed me to spread the work out but also to evaluate each of my custodians and maintenance workers more effectively.

EVALUATING THE PRINCIPAL

I always felt that if I was going to evaluate others, they should get to evaluate me. Twice a year I gathered my department heads and instructed them to call department meetings to evaluate my job through the teachers' eyes. I gave them the following instructions:

1. I am not all good and I am not all bad, so it is important that you tell me what the teachers think I am doing right and what I am doing wrong.

2. Whatever you choose to tell me that I am doing well, I want evidence of.

3. Whatever you choose to tell me that I am doing wrong, I want some form of evidence, and you must suggest a way you would change what I did. In other words, you can't simply complain.

At the next department heads meeting, each department leader reported the results of their discussions. My secretary attended all of the meetings and took down all of the department reports as they were made, then typed them up and gave them to me after the meeting. I was surprised that there were always more things reported that I was doing right than wrong. I responded in writing to each suggestion for change so people knew I listened to their suggestions. Many of the suggestions I was able to implement on the spot.

CONDUCTING MEETINGS

My superintendent appointed me to represent the school district at a series of community meetings searching for a new middle school site. The meetings were from 6:00 PM to 9:00 PM once a week until the job was completed. I cannot tell you how underwhelmed I felt at the honor. I was sure that the meetings would go on forever.

The first night, the chairman called the meeting to order. He told us the purpose and desired outcomes of the meetings and then he pulled a box of breakfast cereal out of a bag and shook it. He said, "Instead of a gavel I chose a box of cereal. Whenever we get off task I will shake it to remind you that if we don't get back to work we may have to stay here until we need to eat it."

Over the years I developed a plan that helped me to expedite meetings and move the groups to effective planning and decision making. The following is a checklist for conducting a meeting:

1. Establish the purpose for the meeting. Make it clear and narrow the focus.

2. Develop outcomes needed to achieve the purpose. These should include the product of the meeting, that is, report, handbook, and so on.

3. Decide who will need to be there and why.

4. Determine the activities needed to reach the outcomes.

5. Make an agenda that reflects Items 1 to 4 and includes dates, time, and location of the meeting. Distribute to all people invited.

6. At the meeting, establish rules for making decisions, attendance, behavior, and so on. Publish and post the rules at each meeting.

7. Facilitate the meeting by adhering to the rules, times, and agenda.

STRANGE THINGS CAN HAPPEN

I will call the woman in this story Ms. Abigail to protect the identity of the actual person.

We had a person in our district, Ms. Abigail, a rather rotund woman, who had to take medication regularly to prevent depression. When she forgot to take her medication, she often did strange things. One of the behaviors she exhibited on those occasions was for her to go to a public place and take off her clothes.

On this particular day, my secretary looked up from her desk and glanced momentarily out the window. Suddenly she shouted, "Good Lord! Ms. Abigail just went into Room 12!" Almost simultaneously, we received a call from the teacher in Room 12, exclaiming, "Send someone quickly. Ms. Abigail just walked into my room."

I leapt from my desk and ran out, not forgetting my radio, toward Room 12. I radioed back as I ran, requesting the police. On entering the room, I encountered the shocked looks of students; a rather perplexed teacher; and Ms. Abigail, already down to her bra and panties, reaching back attempting to remove the bra. Fortunately, my entrance interrupted her and she paused. I said, "Hello, Ms. Abigail. Would you like to step outside with me?" Fortunately, the police entered at this moment. They knew her well. One officer picked up her clothes while the other escorted her out saying, "Forget your medicine again, Ms. Abigail?"

The teacher and I began a discussion with the students about some of the medical and psychological problems people can develop. The discussion included input from the students and turned a possible situation of ridicule into one of empathy.

Another incident occurred on one of those days with the potential for trouble. We had many teachers absent and in their places were some of our very best substitutes. Since we did not have enough experienced subs to go around, we had two who were brand-new to us and one who had never substituted before.

Third period was almost over when a rather distraught child came into the office announcing, "Someone better go down to Room 18 now!"

I recognized that Room 18 was where the inexperienced substitute was working. I took my radio and walked quickly toward the room. As I was approaching, I could see in the open door. All the students were seated rigidly at their desks with their hands folded on the tops. A young man seated near the door caught my eye and urgently motioned with his head for me to come in.

As I entered the dead-quiet room, I was greeted by the view of the substitute totally absorbed with making small erasures on a blackboard covered with student graffiti. As she "touched up" the graffiti she was saying, "This is very important to my work. I must remember it." With that, she saw me and looked into my face with a blank faraway look and said, "I'm going to be killed, you know! All good people are killed and I need to finish my work before they kill me." She then turned her attention to the "art."

I radioed my vice principal and asked him to go to the cafeteria to await the students from her class. I then said to the students, "Lunchtime. Go to the cafeteria." Actually, lunchtime was a period away. Not one student questioned me. They merely stood up and walked quietly to the cafeteria.

I then turned my attention to the teacher, who was totally absorbed with the graffiti. I asked her if she had had a tough day and she replied, "I guess I came out too soon."

After removing her from the room we took her home, where her mother told us that she had been confined to a mental hospital until the week before she started substituting. Lucky us.

Again I spent time with the students from the classes that she had been with. The teacher and I led the students to viewing the person in an empathetic way.

Two weeks later she returned to substitute again. This time I intercepted her and sent her home. I used my report of the incident to have her removed from the substitute rolls.

CONCLUDING THOUGHTS

The final story above emphasizes one reality of being a principal: that no matter how well you are trained, no matter how much you read, and no matter how much experience you have you can never be fully prepared for everything that will happen to you when you are finally in charge of your own school.

The best you can hope for is to know that you are equipped with the ability and the staff to solve the seemingly unsolvable problems, that no matter what happens the kids come in September and go home in June and you didn't just "survive" it all but met the challenges of the year and made a difference for the children in your charge.

This book has provided you with many ideas and stories that we hope will cause you to think deeply and creatively about your own administrative world.

Parting Words of Wisdom   Box 10.1

♦ Always keep the children's best interest foremost in your thoughts and decisions.
♦ Remain flexible; there are exceptions to every rule.
♦ Always be honest and true to yourself.
♦ Strive for simplicity and understanding.
♦ Solicit support; you can't do it all by yourself.
♦ Share your successes as well as your failures.
♦ Have value-based goals for yourself and your school.
♦ Be creative.
♦ Reflect daily.
♦ Be tactful.
♦ Choose your fights carefully.
♦ Put your energy where it counts.
♦ Self-assess.
♦ Pat yourself on the back for a job well done.
♦ Laugh often.
♦ Listen.

♦ Be trusting and trustworthy.

♦ Have a private life.

Remember that schools are wonderful gardens that grow our future. This is a job for people with scope and courage and not for the meek and mild. Administrators have the daunting task of preparing our children to take over from us. What we do today will affect generations to come, and as educators we have the opportunity to develop a dynamic learning culture in our schools.

This philosophy is reflected in the following quote: "Let us as educators not be merchants of facts but instead purveyors of wonderment, vendors of questions and ideas, and incubators of the imagination" (Pat Schumaker, personal communication, 1999).

Resource

Some Must-Read Books
for Administrators: An Annotated List

Arrien, A. (1993). *The four-fold way: Walking paths of the warrior, teacher, healer, and visionary.* New York: HarperCollins.

This is the book I continually reread for inspiration and guidance. Angeles Arrien uses stories and activities from many cultures to demonstrate the need for whole leaders. I highly recommend this book and her workshops. Her basic tenets are

1. Show up and be fully present.
2. Pay attention to what has heart and meaning.
3. Tell the truth without blame or judgment.
4. Be open to outcome, not attached to it.

Buckingham, M., & Coffman, C. (1999). *First, break all the rules.* New York: Simon & Schuster.

This is a book based on interviews with 80,000 managers reporting on what the best managers do differently. One of the author's premises is that people leave managers, not companies. There are 12 questions given in the book that principals may want to use with their staff members. This book will challenge many assumptions and push principals to new thinking over issues.

Cooper, R., & Sawaf, A. (1997). *Executive EQ.* New York: Grosset/Putnam.

The authors have expanded the work of Daniel Goleman on emotional intelligence and made a connection to managers and leaders. They talk about why executives fail and that they do so mainly in the area of emotions. Principals are in an emotional business. The success and stability of principals needs to include a component on emotional intelligence of leaders. There are many exercises and helpful hints throughout the book.

Heuerman, T. C. (1997). *A more natural way: Leadership for sustainable organizations.* Unpublished doctoral dissertation. Available at www. amorenaturalway.com

Tom Heuerman blends chaos theory with the stories of supervisors who demonstrate good results from being authentic leaders. He also publishes a series of pamphlets, at no charge, on his web site. He believes that leaders who work with organizations need to have an "ecological worldview," which includes safety, trust, and being human in the workplace. He works with businesses and schools to develop productive work environments.

Johnson, B. (1992). *Polarity management.* Amherst, MA: HRD.

Most issues principals deal with are not problems to solve, they are polarities to manage. Johnson gives a template you can use to determine the pluses and minuses of a situation. Polarities have two elements: (a) the poles are interdependent, and (b) the issue is ongoing. An example is when a school has a veteran staff, many members of which are retiring, and new people joining the staff; this situation may set up a conflict. Consider what are the best things about the veteran staff and what are the worst? Do the same thing for the young crusaders. Now, how do you, as principal, keep the best of both without staying in the negative territory? A great new tool for principals.

Lambert, L., et al. (1995). *The constructivist leader.* New York: Teachers College Press.

The authors connect constructivist theory to leadership. They identify the necessity for leaders of reflection and the ability to coach yourself and others and include specific examples in schools. The multiple authors provide several viewpoints of leadership and what is required to have a learning organization in schools.

Palmer, P. (1998). *The courage to teach.* San Francisco: Jossey-Bass.

The author talks about teachers' personal and professional lives. This was the first book I read that actually talked about our identity as educators, what that means for us, and the need to integrate our work and personal lives. The chapter on the "culture of fear" particularly impressed me. Palmer's work has huge implications for developing a safe, trustful culture for educators to work in and live in.

Payne, R. K. (1995). *A framework: Understanding and working with students and adults from poverty.* Baytown, TX: RFT Publishing. 1-800-424-9484

Schools are getting more and more diverse. Socioeconomic diversity is extremely influential in our ability to teach children from poverty. This book leads the way for urban, rural, and suburban issues schools are dealing with and will continue to deal with from our families. Poverty continues to mount and the effects on schools will cause us to do things differently. This book was called a must-read at the NSDC convention.

Stewart, T. A. (1997). *Intellectual capital.* New York: Doubleday-Currency.

W. B. Yeats said, "Education is not a pail to fill, it is a fire to light." As we move from the empty vessel metaphor of schools to the ability to use and make meaning from information, Stewart gives us a different model to look at. How do we capitalize on the intellectual skills of students, teachers, and principals? He suggests we need to look at three things: human capital, structural capital, and customer capital. I think this may be the metaphor for schools of the future.

Tichy, N. (1997). *The leadership engine.* New York: HarperCollins.

Two major themes are present in this book: (a) leaders must be learners in times of major change, for relying on old methods may not get the desired outcome; and (b) a major task of leaders is to develop more leaders. Even though I have mentored many educators who wanted to be administrators, I never really thought that was part of my job. This book provides a different look at leadership.

References and Further Reading

Ackoff, R. L. (1991). *Ackoff's fables.* New York: John Wiley.

Arin-Krupp, J. (1987, October). *Motivating the adult learner.* ASCD workshop, Minneapolis, MN.

Atwell, N. (1988). *In the middle: New understanding about writing, reading and learning.* San Francisco: Greenwood-Heineman.

Autry, J. (1991). *Love and profit: The art of caring leadership.* New York: Avon.

Bardwick, J. M. (1986). *The plateauing trap.* New York: Bantam.

Barth, R. S. (1990). *Improving schools from within.* San Francisco: Jossey-Bass.

Bennis, W. (1989). *Why leaders can't lead.* San Francisco: Jossey-Bass.

Bennis, W. (1997). *Managing people is like herding cats.* Provo, UT: Executive Excellence Publishing.

Bennis, W., & Nanus, B. (1985). *Leaders.* New York: Harper & Row.

Berliner, D., & Biddle, B. (1995). *The manufactured crisis.* Reading, MA: Addison-Wesley.

Bernstein, A. J., & Rozen, S. C. (1989). *Dinosaur brains.* New York: Ballantine.

Block, P. (1987). *The empowered manager.* San Francisco: Jossey-Bass.

Bode, R. (1993). *First you have to row a little boat.* New York: Warner.

Bohm, D. (1989, November 6). *On dialogue.* Notes from seminar in Ojai, CA.

Bolman, L. G., & Deal, T. E. (1995). *Leading with soul.* San Francisco: Jossey-Bass.

Bridges, W. (1991). *Managing transitions: Making the most of change.* New York: Addison-Wesley.

Byham, W. C. (1992). *Zapp! in education*. New York: Fawcett.

Carlzon, J. (1987). *Moments of truth*. New York: Harper & Row.

Carse, J. P. (1986). *Finite and infinite games*. Ballantine.

Collins, J., & Porras, J. (1994). *Built to last*. New York: HarperCollins.

Costa, A. L., & Garmston, R. J. (1994). *Cognitive Coaching: A foundation for renaissance schools*. Norwood, NJ: Christopher-Gordon.

Covey, S. R., et al. (1994). *First things first*. New York: Simon & Schuster.

Crum, T. F. (1987). *The magic of conflict*. New York: Touchstone Books, Simon & Schuster.

Deming, W. E. (n.d.). *The five deadly sins*. Videotape.

Fassel, D. (1990). *Working ourselves to death*. New York: HarperCollins.

Fisher, R., & Ury, W. (1981). *Getting to yes*. Penguin.

Fulghum, R. (1993). *All I really need to know I learned in kindergarten: Uncommon thoughts on common things*. New York: Fawcett.

Fullan, M. (1993). *Change forces*. London: Falmer.

Gardner, J. (1990). *On leadership*. New York: Free Press.

Gardner, J. W. (1963). *Self-renewal*. New York: Harper & Row.

Garfield, C. (1986). *Peak performers*. New York: Avon.

Goleman, D. (1995). *Emotional intelligence*. New York: Bantam.

Hoff, R. (1988). *I can see you naked*. Kansas City: A Universal Press.

Johnson, S. M. (1990). *Teachers at work*. New York: Basic Books.

Joyce, B., & Showers, B. (1988). *Student achievement through staff development*. White Plains, NY: Longman.

Kohn, A. (1993). *Punished by rewards: The trouble with gold stars, incentive plans, A's, praise, and other bribes*. New York: Houghton Mifflin.

Kouzes, J. M., & Posner, B. Z. (1993). *Credibility*. San Francisco: Jossey-Bass.

Lambert, L., Walker, D., Zimmerman, D. P., Cooper, J. P., Lambert, M .D., Gardner, M. E., & Ford Slack, P. J. (1995). *The construcivist leader*. New York: Teachers College Press.

Lynch, D., & Kordis, P. (1988). *Strategy of the dolphin*. New York: Fawcett Columbine.

Machado, L. A. (1980). *The right to be intelligent*. Oxford, UK: Pergamon Press.

Maslow, A. (1987). *Motivation and personality* (3rd ed.). New York, NY: Wiley & Sons.

Maslow, A. (1998). In R. E. Lowery (Ed.), *Toward a psychology of being* (3rd ed.). New York: Wiley & Sons.

Merriam, S. B. (1993). *An update on adult learning theory.* San Francisco: Jossey-Bass.

Miller, L. M. (1989). *Barbarians to bureaucrats.* New York: Fawcett.

Pascale, R. T. (1990). *Managing on the edge.* New York: Simon & Schuster.

Payne, R. K. (1995). *A framework: Understanding and working with students and adults from poverty.* Baytown, TX: RFT Publishing.

Perkins, D. (1992). *Smart schools.* New York: Free Press.

Rosenholtz, S. J. (1989). *Teachers' workplace.* New York: Longman.

Schön, D. (1983). *The reflective practitioner.* New York: Basic Books.

Seligman, M.E.P. (1990). *Learned optimism.* New York: Knopf.

Senge, P. M. (1992). *The fifth discipline.* New York: Doubleday Current.

Sergiovanni, T. (1994). *Building community in schools.* San Francisco: Jossey-Bass.

Stacey, R. D. (1997). *Managing the unknowable.* San Francisco: Jossey-Bass.

Stewart, T. A. (1997). *Intellectual capital.* New York: Doubleday-Currency.

Ury, W. (1991). *Getting past no.* New York: Bantam.

Waber, B. (1972). *Ira sleeps over.* Boston: Houghton Mifflin.

Wheatley, M. J. (1992). *Leadership and the new science.* San Francisco: Berrett-Koehler.

Wheatley, M., & Kellner-Rogers, M. (1996). *A simpler way.* San Francisco: Berrett-Koehler.

Whyte, D. (1994). *The heart aroused.* New York: Currency/Doubleday.

Index

personal support systems,
140-143
process of education and, 27-32

Undermining types, 81, 82-83
Unity, assumption of, 98-99
Unpopular decisions, 109-112

Values. *See* Beliefs and values
Vandalism, 154-155

Video cameras, use of, 154-155

Web pages, school, 13
Whole language approach, 65
Words of wisdom, 165-166
Work load and power, demands of,
147-149
Work request forms, 160-161
Workshops, coaching, 103